A Starfarer's dozen.

DATE			

A STARFARER'S DOZEN

A STARFARER'S DOZEN

Stories of Things to Come

EDITED BY

MICHAEL STEARNS

ILLUSTRATED BY

MICHAEL HUSSAR

Jane Yolen Books
Harcourt Brace & Company
San Diego New York London

Library of Congress Cataloging-in-Publication Data
A starfarer's dozen: stories of things to come/edited by Michael Stearns; illustrated by Michael Hussar.
p. cm.
"Jane Yolen books."
Companion to A wizard's dozen.
Contents: Jones and the stray/Martha Soukup—Ursa Minor/Gregory Feeley—Secret Identity/Will Shetterly—Suraki/Dave Trowbridge—On perdition/Dan Bennett—Crossover/Debra Doyle and James D. Macdonald—Exchange student/Janni Lee Simner—Wilding/Jane Yolen—Vet-o-saurus/Joy Oestreicher—Celestial debris/Lawrence Watt-Evans—Flyboy/Deborah Coates—I was a teenage superhero/Sherwood Smith—We don't know why/Nancy Springer.
ISBN 0-15-299871-3
1. Science fiction, American. 2. Children's stories, American.
[1. Science fiction. 2. Short stories.] I. Stearns, Michael. II. Hussar, Michael, ill.
PZ5.S796 1995
813'.0876208
[Fic]—dc20 95-8455

The text was set in Sabon.
Designed by Linda Lockowitz and Trina Stahl
Printed in the United States of America

First edition

A B C D E

For the Travelin' Sooz,

wherever that great heart may now be

star•far•er's doz•en \ 'stär-ˌfar-erz 'dəz-ən \ *n* [origin unknown] (ca. 2041)

1 : any number between eleven and fifteen **2** *slang* : nickname for a group spacewalk, usually composed of adolescents **3** *slang* : number of solo outings required before a cadet earns the rank of *starfarer*

WITHOUT WHOM, &c.

In the haste of putting together *A Wizard's Dozen*, the first volume in this series, a number of invaluable contributors were overlooked. So, belated thanks to Michael Hussar for the art in that book and this one, and for the good grace he showed not to complain when his illustration credit vanished; to Trina Stahl for the eye-catching design; to Karen Weller-Watson for indescribable help and endless good taste; to Gordon Van Gelder for acknowledged assistance; and lastly, for the idea of the anthologies, for her proddings and editorial suggestions—for everything, in short, except the mistakes—thanks to the grand matron of the imprint, Jane Yolen. She let me stay out late with this one, and I am grateful.

CONTENTS

TO THE STARS!

If a seafarer travels across oceans, then perhaps a starfarer journeys between planets and stars. But actual travel to distant worlds hasn't really begun yet, except in its simplest forms. There have been spacewalks and moon landings and the regular thunder of rockets rising into blue skies, but for the most part, we are still earthbound. No matter—a starfarer doesn't let gravity's pull keep her at home.

And why should she? Starfaring isn't simply about *travel*—that's just a small part of it. Starfaring begins before travel, before even the first rocket is built, and it has been taking place for as long as there have been dreamers. This kind of starfaring is the dream of exploration—not only the exploration of new places, but new directions of every sort. The future is not only Out There, it is also in the here and now. When everyone else is looking at the horizon, the starfarer looks up, looks down, looks *in,* and says, "That way!"

Explorers may be the first to go somewhere, but their *desires* to go are first fired by the tales they've grown up with. It was so with seafaring: Columbus was inspired by the fantastic tales of Marco Polo. In the same way, tomorrow's astronauts will have dreamed possible futures in the pages of science fiction, trying a dozen different tomorrows in books by Heinlein and Le Guin, Asimov and Bradbury and others. That is where they will have learned the first rule of starfaring: that you can't get there from here without imagination.

The futuristic desire to go "to the stars" is really not so different from the centuries-old command to "go forth," no different from what makes any explorer leave her home. At its purest level, starfaring is about *hope*—hope of finding something better out there, or something that is missing here, or maybe just something *else*. The odd thing is that everyone who sets off into the great unknown, the wide world, the Out There, ends up discovering herself.

And that is what the best science fiction is all about.

A STARFARER'S DOZEN

MARTHA SOUKUP

JONES AND THE STRAY

Jones blew hard to see how far out her breath would fog. Pretty far. It seemed to her it must be possible—if the wind were still and there were the same amount of moisture in the air—to guess the temperature by the length of the breath cloud you could blow. If you filled your lungs with the same amount of air and blew just as hard.

Well, that was an awful lot of ifs. Maybe not.

When you were in Alaska in the winter, you always knew it was cold, anyway, and you'd better never let yourself forget it if you wanted to stay alive.

She was rattling at the doorknob of her warehouse. Jones called it her warehouse; whoever's warehouse it actually was wasn't using it for anything. It was a small, wind-leaky, smelly building, thrown together years ago out of corrugated steel.

What was important was that no one had ever turned off the electricity, and that the lock would give if you jiggled it just right. Of course she didn't have the key.

"Come on, door," Jones said, making two more puffs of frosty breath that drifted back past her ear.

The doorknob felt cold even through the glove of her heatsuit. The suit's charge was wearing down. She'd taken off the big knit glove she usually wore over the thin heatsuit glove, and was holding it in the other knit glove. She wore lots of layers of wool and polyester over the suit, to hold in heat and save the charge. And to make her look bigger, and more anonymous.

She had brought the heatsuit with her from Seattle, along with all the money she had been able to scrounge in a hurry. That was all she had when she left. Her name she acquired a day or two later. She made it up on the long bus trip north, right after she cut her hair short and shaggy in a diner restroom. "Jones." If you said it fast and gruff, maybe no one'd notice exactly who was under all those clothes, especially if you were tall for your age.

Not if you didn't give them too much time to look at you.

"Come on!" she whispered urgently, and the lock slipped, the door opened.

She gave one quick glance behind her and ducked inside.

It was even darker here than it was outside. A little bit of moonlight came in through the cracks in the wall panels. Jones found the light switch. She crossed her fingers, hoping the lights would come on. They did. There was still electricity.

It was funny how you never noticed how tight your shoulders were until they relaxed. Jones turned the lights off again quickly, so that no one would see them, and hurried to the far corner of the warehouse. She felt with her hand for the electrical outlet. With her other hand she took the heavy square transformer from one of her many pockets. She plugged the little lead from the transformer into the suit's connector under her armpit. She plugged the big lead into the electrical outlet in the concrete floor.

She lay back awkwardly against the crinkled wall. The heatsuit wasn't really designed to be recharged while you were still wearing it. You were supposed to be indoors someplace warm, letting it charge back up overnight on a table somewhere while you were in a nice soft bed under all the covers.

Jones reached inside her layers of clothes to a big pocket and found dinner, a plastic bag from inside a cereal box, half-full of puffed corn. She leaned on her left elbow and started eating it with her right hand. The crunch of the cereal was loud and satisfying. She settled in and let her gaze drift across the blackness.

A pair of eyes was looking at her from the near corner of the warehouse.

Jones gasped before she could stop it and clutched

her cereal bag close. She drew herself up against the wall as far as she could without unplugging herself, and felt inside her pockets for the long steel wrench she carried there.

"Who's there?" she said loudly in her deepest, gruffest growl.

Silence for a moment.

"Bad," came a thin little voice. "Bad run bad boy hungry food stay away food."

"What?" said Jones, forgetting for a moment in her surprise to use her Jones voice. She found the wrench.

"Bad," the voice said again. "Bad boy dangerous stay away bite bad food hungry food please."

It didn't sound like a man's voice or a woman's voice or a kid's voice. It sounded like a computer, like the computer in class when she still went to school, or the computer her friend Cary used to play games on. Under the voice she could hear the wet sound of heavy breathing.

The eyes were big and round, with a greenish blue glow in the tiny glint of moonlight. They blinked and stared at her.

Jones thought he must have been in there much longer than she'd been, and his eyes would be better adjusted; but no one could see very well in here. She yanked the plug from her suit, dropped her food, and stood with the wrench held high, trying to look big in all her clothes.

"Leave now and there won't be trouble!" she cried in her best mean man's voice.

He barked. Jones almost dropped the wrench.

"Go away go away bad bite bad boy bad dog mean bite go," said the thin computer voice.

"Dog?" said Jones. She squinted, and could barely make out its shaggy gray shape. Lowering the wrench, but holding it tightly, she took a step forward.

The dog whined, and at the same time the voice said, "Bad go scared go bad bad bad bite food please scared." It scrunched back as far as it could go in the corner, whimpering.

"Poor dog," Jones said. "Poor thing, I won't hurt you."

Now she could make out its voder collar. She'd seen rich people walking poodles that were wearing those. The collars had little computers in them that could translate a dog's brain waves into words. It took a lot of training for dogs to use them, and they were expensive. This dog seemed, in the gloom, as scruffy and scared as any stray she'd ever seen, but it must have a rich owner, to afford both the collar and the genetic work that improved its verbal skills so it could use it. She took another slow step forward.

The dog whimpered again. It said, through the collar, "Back bad mean dog bite bite back." Then it moaned and said, "Scared hungry scared."

"It's okay," she said gently. She walked backward, feeling for the cereal bag with her foot. She put the wrench on the floor and took a handful of cereal, holding it out in front of her. "See? Here's some food. It's okay."

The dog was silent, but it stared at her hand.

Jones crouched down, tiptoeing on her haunches to the dog, with the food held out. Now she was right in front of it.

The dog was so still it could have been a stuffed animal. Its eyes looked up from the food to her face. "It's okay," she said, almost whispering. "It's okay. I'm a friend. It's okay."

The dog didn't take its eyes off hers, but then its muzzle was in her hand, its breath warm and moist through the mesh of her heatsuit glove. It licked and ate up the cereal with delicate little movements of its mouth, staring at her.

"See? It's okay. I'm a friend." She reached out to touch its head and the dog ducked away. Jones felt hurt. Then she thought it must still be scared. "It's okay," she said again. She dug through her pockets and found some pretzels, and put them on the floor in front of the dog. "You can have whatever you want."

The dog ate the pretzels. She watched. She could see it better, now that she was close and her eyes had adjusted. It was one of those pretty white dogs. She knew their name: a Samoyed. When they were puppies they looked like toys, with their black button eyes and their fluffy fur and tails. This one was not a little puppy, but it was not full grown, and its fur was dingy and matted with dirt.

"I'm Jones," she said to the dog. "Jones." She patted her chest.

The dog finished eating. It looked at her again. "Ohnz," it said.

"Jones."

"Gohnz. Ohnz. Bones."

Jones laughed. "Not bones. Jones."

"Shones. Jones."

"Jones. Good, yes, Jones."

Carefully, Jones reached out and stroked its head. The dog let her do it. Encouraged, she rubbed its ear and neck. She couldn't remember the last time she'd petted a dog. But there weren't a lot of nice things she remembered—and plenty of things she didn't intend to remember—from before she'd left Seattle.

The dog yelped. She pulled back her hand. "What's wrong?" There was something sticky on her glove. She looked at it. "You're bleeding!"

"Hurt run away bad boy hurt," the dog said. She reached to see where the blood was. The dog cringed away.

"It's okay," Jones said. "I'm your friend. I want to see where you're hurt."

She put her hand on its neck and pulled the dog gently around to look at its other side. It whimpered softly, and its collar said, "Hurt bad no please," but it let her do it.

A piece of the dog's skin hung, torn and wet looking, from its flank. Jones's throat felt funny when she saw it; she had to swallow, hard. She made herself look. It was roughly the shape of a triangle, torn from the top, hanging down at the bottom. The flank where the skin had ripped was raw and unpleasant to see.

"What happened?" she asked the dog. "How did you do this? How did you hurt yourself?"

"Hurt," the dog said. It had stopped whimpering, and it looked at her as though it expected something. "Hurt."

"How did you hurt yourself?" she asked again.

"Run away bad dog," it said. "Run away bad master. Hide. Hide inside catch hurt catch pull hurt."

"Catch what? Hurt where?"

The dog looked along the wall of the warehouse toward the door. She looked where it was looking, and could see, just a few feet away, that a join where two sheets of steel had been welded together had come loose. The tear in the wall was only a few inches wide. The dog must have forced its way in through it.

"Did you hurt yourself coming through that hole?" She pointed. "That hole? That hole hurt you?"

"Yes hurt hide inside hide run away yes."

"You poor thing," Jones said again. She hugged it around the neck, hearing its breath in her ear. "Poor dog, why are you hiding?"

"Hide."

"Why?"

"Bad dog run away hide."

"I don't think you're a bad dog," Jones said. When the dog heard "bad dog" it cringed. "No no," she said. "Good dog. You're a good dog. Why did you run away?"

"Hit bad dog hit shout hit run away run away," the dog said.

"Did your master hit you?" Jones asked, feeling her cheeks burn with outrage. Just thinking of it made her want to hit someone back, though she'd promised herself she would never do that.

"Hit bad dog," it said.

"Bad master," Jones said. Her eyes stung.

"Bad master," said the dog.

She made herself calm down. She didn't want to upset the dog. She petted it quietly for a while. "We have to get you fixed," she said. She winced. "Not *fixed* fixed, I mean we have to get your wound fixed."

"Fix," said the dog. "Help."

"I don't know how to get you help," Jones said. She remembered a veterinary clinic a little to the side of town. How could she just go in there with a runaway dog—her, a runaway herself? They wouldn't be open until morning anyway.

"Jones fix," said the dog.

"Oh, no," Jones said. "I can't fix it." Runaway kids were sent home. Her face was probably on milk cartons. They could look inside their databanks and figure out where to send her back. Freezing in a shed would be better than that.

"Jones fix."

"Sweetie, I don't know how to, I don't have medicine and tools, I can't do it, honey—what is your name?"

The dog was quiet.

"Your name?" Jones said, very clearly.

"Name no. Master shout name bad bad name no. Name bad."

That was almost funny. "You and me, we've got a lot in common. Should I give you a name? Do you want to pick a name?"

The dog looked confused. "Jones fix."

"Okay," Jones said. "Um. Okay. Um. How about Diogenes? He went away from home to find an honest man. I read it in a book about old Greek philosophers. They didn't say if he ever found one." The dog put its head in her lap. "Diogenes?" She said it slowly and carefully: *Dye Ah John Eez.*

The dog tried the name. "Ah geez."

"Ah-geez," Jones agreed. It wasn't the dumbest name she'd ever heard, and the dog was the only one in the world who had it.

"Cold," said Ah-geez. "Hurt cold." The computer voice was calm and ordinary, every word coming out the same. But the dog was beginning to tremble.

"Oh, lord," said Jones. "I can't do anything until morning. What if you've gotten infected? I think if you're sick you have to be specially careful to stay warm." The dog's pelt looked warm, but the place it was torn looked fragile and dangerous. With her heatsuit still working, covering her up from her toes to most of her face, she hadn't thought how painful the freezing air would be on the wound. "Okay," she said. "Okay."

She took off all her many layers of clothes, from the biggest on the outside to the smallest on the inside. She unzipped her heatsuit. The cold air hit her like a fist. "Oh my pete's sake geez!" she said. She hurried back into all her other clothes. It was cold without the heatsuit. She wondered if she could get through a night that cold.

"Here you go," she said. "You have to help me get this over you."

Ah-geez looked uncomprehending, but when she lifted the dog up to try to get its back legs into the legs of the suit, it shifted itself around to help. She pulled the suit up slowly. When she got to the torn part, she winced and put the skin back carefully in place, figuring it had to be less dirty than the inside of her suit. Ah-geez yelped when she touched the wound, then was still, breathing hard.

Jones got the front legs into the heatsuit's arms. She left the suit's hood and mask down, since they wouldn't fit over a dog's face. It all made a lumpy weird shape, a lumpy shape she was perhaps the first person ever to discover. Dog inside heatsuit.

"Better?" she asked.

"No cold," Ah-geez said.

"Good," she said.

"Good Jones Jones good," the dog said.

"You're welcome," she said. "Now we wait until morning, and then I'll think of something."

Shivering, she huddled up against the dog's unwounded side and waited for the next dark morning. The dog slept, kicking softly, as dogs do, when it dreamed.

Jones fought to stay awake. She kept watch all night, just like hundreds of nights in Seattle, worrying her way into the next day.

The sun didn't come up properly in Alaska in the winter. It clung to the horizon, like sunrise all day. So the streetlights were on and it still felt like night when Jones struggled toward the vet clinic, arms full of lumpy dog.

She wished the streetlights would just short out, make everything as dark as could be. She felt obvious and exposed, everything she had run north not to be.

Mostly she felt exhausted. She could carry Ah-geez, but the dog felt heavier with every step she took. She couldn't shift her arms around without worrying about hurting the torn part of its flank.

She had turned the suit off before leaving the shed,

but the dog still felt hot, very hot, too hot. That was what had made up her mind. Ah-geez was sick. There had to be an infection for the dog to be that hot, so much hotter than when she had first found it.

A woman was unlocking the door of the clinic when Jones staggered up. She turned and saw Jones and her bundle. "Good morning," she said, as though a skinny shortish person in a lot of clothes, carrying a misshapen bulk of heatsuit with a dog's head panting out of it, was a sight she saw every day.

"Hi," said Jones, and was terrified. She forced her nerves down. "Are you the animal doctor?"

"I am," said the woman. "Doctor Kozlowski. Is that your dog?"

"No," said Jones. "Yes. I mean—" She'd had something all planned out to say, something to maybe throw them off and keep them from looking for her before she could be on a bus and going somewhere else. But it all fell out of her mind. Months of not talking to anyone, silently spending her last dollars on food to supplement what she could scavenge, ducking through the streets trying to look dangerous the rest of the time. She'd forgotten how to talk to people. "He's hurt. I think he's sick, too."

"You'd better come inside," Dr. Kozlowski said. Jones found herself inside and in a bright little examining room in what seemed like four or five steps. She kept her eye on the door.

"What's your name?" the veterinarian asked the dog, noting the voder collar. She was stripping off the suit with sure, efficient hands.

The dog lay panting and didn't answer. "Ah-geez," Jones said.

The vet looked surprised. "How do you spell that?"

"I haven't any idea," Jones said. She stood by the examining-room door, calculating the fastest way out of the building.

"He's not your dog, is he? Did you find him?"

Jones wouldn't give her any clues. She shoved her hands in her pockets and waited, glancing at the door.

"You did a good job, keeping him warm. This must hurt him, here." Dr. Kozlowski examined the wound with gentle fingers. "I'll give him a shot of antibiotic and clean this up, and then we should be able to sew it back where it belongs." She shook her head, looking at the damage. "I'll need to find his owner."

Jones had been waiting for a moment when the vet was distracted, to make her dash, but when she heard this she cried, "No!"

The vet frowned. "No?" Her fingers moved across Ah-geez's dirty fur, pulling it this way and that like an outfielder looking for a softball in tall grass. "Ah. This dog has been hit," she said to herself. "There, there. Another scar there. Oh yes. Creep."

"You'll take care of him?" Jones asked. *Oh, please,* she thought. *Don't send him back.*

"This dog has been hit, and I don't think he's been fed enough. And he's still a puppy. No, I don't think I'll be sending him back where he came from," Dr. Kozlowski said. "We'll take care of him." She was preparing a needle now.

"I can't pay you," Jones said.

"Don't worry about that," said the vet. "I'm on the animal-protection board. I'm their consulting veterinarian. We do that. You did a good thing, bringing Ah-geez—Ah-geez?—here."

"Um. Thanks." The vet was putting the needle under the dog's skin; Ah-geez twitched. Jones inched toward the chair over which the vet had draped her heatsuit.

"Jones help," said the dog in its thin voder voice. "Jones hurt help." Jones was stealthily lifting her suit from the chair. She froze.

"Your friend?" the woman said. "Yes, she helped you."

"Jones," the computer voice said insistently. "Jones Jones Jones hurt Jones hurt. Jones hurt help cry. Bad master hit Jones Jones asleep cry. Cry asleep cry bad master."

She had not! Jones thought, flushing. She'd been awake all night, watching over Ah-geez. She thought. Anyway, maybe she had nightmares about—all that. A long time ago. But she didn't cry in her sleep, not ever, not asleep or awake. She couldn't afford to let anyone know what the tears were about.

Not even a dog. But she must have fallen asleep from exhaustion without realizing it, so exhausted she talked in her sleep. The vet would figure out she was a runaway, and then—

The door was very far away. She had to get out before everything fell apart.

The vet was cleaning the wound, and she didn't look at Jones. She said, in the same calm voice in which she'd talked about antibiotics and stitches, "Sometimes when a dog gets hit enough, he thinks anyone he sees is going to hit him." The vet touched the dog's torn flesh quickly but gently, sponging it clean. "Rotten thing. Most people who hit dogs don't bring them to me, but I see them too often anyway."

Jones was almost to the door. *Squeeze out through it and run until you can't run anymore,* she told herself. It was the only plan she could think of.

"So then there's a dog thinks everyone is going to hit him. But not everyone hits dogs." She looked, then, at Jones, who was stuck in the doorway as though it were only inches wide. "You didn't." Then she said, "If you're brave, and you find the right person, they won't send you back to anyone who hurts you."

"Help Jones help good Jones good help," said the dog. He looked up at the vet and the vet nodded at him, as though she understood everything, though she couldn't possibly.

Jones was dismayed when she felt tears standing in her eyes, embarrassed when Dr. Kozlowski put a hand on her shoulder and walked her gently back inside. "It will help your friend," the vet said in a matter-of-fact way, "if you stroke his head so he knows he has a friend here while I'm sewing this up."

So that's what Jones did.

GREGORY FEELEY

URSA MINOR

At first he thought the whole world had blown up; and then he thought that perhaps only the Forest part of it had; and then he thought that perhaps only he *had, and he was now alone in the moon or somewhere, and would never see Christopher Robin or Pooh or Eeyore again. And then he thought, "Well, even if I'm in the moon, I needn't be face downwards all the time. . . ."*

—A. A. MILNE

". . . only a Bear of Very Little Brain," he concluded helpfully.

"Sixteen teraflops, to be precise," said the man, who had moved behind Edward and was doing something to the back of his head. "That's even stupider than my niece's Talking Book back home. Unfortunately, you're all that we've got."

The man faced Edward again, studying him speculatively. Edward noticed a smudge on the man's forehead and saw that his collar was torn. He usually reminded little people when they needed a wash, but rarely adults, especially when they wore grave expressions.

"Emergency override twenty-six zee lambda," the man said again. Edward looked at him with the affectionate expression he always bore, save when a situation called for gravity. The man sighed. "So you've lost that, too. I don't know if you're damaged beyond reliability or simply too old to conform to regulations."

Edward held forth his right paw, which was charred at the end. "Maybe you should wrap it with a handkerchief. Then I should go see the doctor." He knew immediately that this was inappropriate for a big person, but the correct response was slow in coming. Much of Edward's memory seemed to resist coming into focus.

The man brushed the border of singed fur with a finger. "Some old synthetic, or maybe real, I don't know. Virtually nonconducting, plus the old quilts you were stored with . . ." He shook his head. "Too simpleminded to be damaged, even in a calamity like this."

The physical contact prompted some recollection. "Where is Clive? He must be wondering where I am."

The man grinned. "Gone back to bloody England,

or maybe Mars. Long ago." He asked something Edward could not understand. "No? Then you've only got me to talk to. Not the kind of accent you're used to, eh?"

Edward was too polite to comment on people's accents. "If Clive has gone, I shall have to wait for him."

"You're going to do more than that." The man picked up Edward and propelled himself with a kick through the doorway. "You will do as I say, right? Despite the lack of command override?"

"I always do as I'm told." Tucked under the man's arm, Edward could see nothing. The air was filled with sharp odors, several of which would normally suggest that Clive had spilled something.

Edward was handed to somebody who held him upside down for a moment before setting him on a table. A tired-looking woman studied him for several seconds, poked at his stubby paws, then slipped something around his neck.

Edward looked down at the device, which rested like a pendant on his chest. "Can you hear me, Bear?" it said in the man's voice.

"Oh, yes."

He was picked up again, shaken violently, then thrown against a wall. Edward raised his arms, taking the impact on nose, forepaws, and tummy. Someone snagged his leg as he rebounded. Edward heard the man and woman speak, then the man said in English, "You still okay?"

Edward said he was. They made him walk across the tabletop, then demagnetize the plates beneath his paw pads for a moment and swim through the air. Finally they set him back on the table and asked him several questions. He could do the sums (he had been trained to help Clive on these) but did not know what day of the week it was or what the Sinclairs had had to eat last night. Edward began to explain that he really must be a Bear of Very Little Brain, but the frowning man interrupted.

"You'll have to do." The woman said something, but he cut her off with a word. "Just do exactly what I tell you." His voice was coming from the device again, sounding tiny and flat.

They took him through chambers that, if Clive's, would have prompted his mother to order them cleaned up at once. A young man, dark skinned like the others but with his arm and face bandaged, stared at Edward through his uncovered eye. It began to dawn on Edward that there had been a bad accident.

Edward was held by the scruff and pointed toward a doorway that had buckled sideways. The crumpled door filled the frame save for an isosceles wedge at the apex of one bent jamb.

"Can you get through there?" the man asked as Edward approached the opening and peered in.

"I can certainly try," Edward said. He raised his paws as the man pushed unhelpfully against his bottom, and he began to twist through. His tummy caught almost immediately, but Edward knew its resiliency and squeezed hard. His head emerged into the darkness beyond, and something struck his ear. "Oh, bother!" he cried.

Debris was tumbling through the unlit room, an unsafe situation that Edward knew wasn't allowed. He batted at something that brushed against his muzzle, and a globule of sticky liquid smeared over his fur. "Bother," he said again, then remembered that no one was there to hear him. He kicked his stubby legs to gain purchase, and with a hard push from behind he was through.

Edward rolled lazily through the air, feeling bits of stuff collide with him in the darkness. "Are you through?" the pendant demanded.

"I am indeed." Edward brushed against a wall and quickly swung a leg around to click his sole against it. He stood up carefully, looking across the room at the tiny slice of light.

A beam shone through, filled with swirling objects. "There is a ventilation hatch in the far corner," the pendant told him. "Find it and remove the grille."

Edward worked slowly, using the tiny tools extruded from his left paw to pry off the hatch. The beam of light could not reach this end of the room, but its dusty diffusion sufficed for Edward's eyes. The hatch came free with a soft clang. "Is it off?" the pendant asked. "Now crawl in."

An oily draft puffed against his face. "It's rather cold," Edward remarked. Temperature extremes did not bother him, but he was sensitive to children's comfort.

The man laughed. "It will get a lot colder."

Edward crawled through the narrow shaft, leaving the dim light behind. A safety feature of his design heightened alertness in novel situations, and Edward's sensorium quivered at its maximum sensitivity.

"There should be an opening ahead on your left," the pendant said. "Continue past it." Other turnings were ignored or taken, at the man's direction. Edward came at last to another grille, through which no light shone. At a touch it came off, drifting into the darkness beyond to clang against unseen walls.

Edward found the far door with difficulty and had to feel along its frame to locate the manual switch. "It doesn't appear to work," he reported. The man swore unintelligibly, then came back after a minute with instructions for sliding the door open. Edward dutifully braced his paws against the frame and clamped his soles to the door, but he was able to move it only a few centimeters. "This is a job for a big person," he said.

"Wedge your arms into the opening," the pendant told him. "Move them back and forth." A sliver of gray light had appeared. Edward worked steadily until he felt his servomotors begin to strain. "That doesn't matter," the operator told him. "Press your head in and use your neck motors. Squeeze in your shoulders, then push."

Edward forced his head and arms through the opening, then brought all four limbs up against the door. It slid several centimeters, under increasing resistance, as though one of its runners were bent.

The hallway beyond was lined with floor strips that glowed in the absence of regular lighting. When Edward turned slightly to gain a better vantage, he saw the body. It floated unmoving, legs drawn up as though in sleep. "I think someone's hurt," Edward said.

"Anybody still there is past hurting. Continue with your work."

"You should bring help right away." Although Edward could not experience distress, the sight had boosted his operating system into such urgency that his voice emerged strained.

"Listen, Bear, help is coming. Pay no attention to

anything but your task." The voice was speaking slowly and clearly. "Help is *on its way* for that poor person, do you understand?"

Slowly Edward turned his head back to the doorway in which he was wedged. He strained against it until he felt his motors race close to their limits, then began pushing himself through. His tummy, scraped clean of fur, emerged with a series of short squeaks.

"You in? Proceed down the hallway to the end. Keep your eyes on the glowing strips; look at nothing else."

Edward pulled himself paw over paw along the floor, intent on avoiding the objects that tumbled past his peripheral vision. The air was very bad; if Clive appeared Edward would have to send him straight home.

At the end of the hallway the voice told Edward to look for a sign that read SERVICE MODULE. "I can read," Edward said helpfully. "Reading is easy and fun."

"Not if the emergency subsystems are knocked out, too," the voice from the pendant said irritably.

"I see it!" cried Edward. "The letters are flickering."

"Flickering? That's not good." For a minute the man seemed to be speaking with someone else, using words Edward couldn't understand. Then he asked, "Can you reach the control pad?"

Edward was not supposed to touch strange control pads, and Clive wasn't, either. "If you want me to," he said doubtfully. He climbed the wall on his magnetized soles and tapped the pad three times. One of the twin panels underneath slid open, but the other didn't move.

"Shine a light inside," the voice told him after Edward explained this. Edward activated a penlight in his right paw and played its beam over the circuitry within. Even he could tell that something was wrong; many of the modular units were hanging at odd angles or trailing wires, and some of their casings were cracked.

"Describe everything you see, from left to right," the voice said. This took quite awhile, because Edward did not know much about electronics, and the voice frequently asked him to go back and explain something in greater detail.

"What a mess," the man said when Edward had finished.

"Perhaps I could help you clean up," said Edward dutifully. "Cleaning up can be fun."

"You don't clean up after this kind of accident; you just try to survive it." The voice sighed. "Okay, let's see what you can do."

At the voice's direction, Edward found a storage locker farther down the hall, which he had to open by hand. He read out the components arrayed inside—"Good thing they're still labeled in English, eh, Eduardo?" the man asked—and found two small flat rectangles that bore the numbers the man wanted. He pulled them out, holding them clumsily in his stubby paws, and walked along the wall back to the service module.

"Do you see a row of cassettes just like the ones you're holding? Look to the left."

Edward looked carefully. "There are nine of them," he pronounced.

"Good. Pull out the second and eighth ones."

Though Edward was not very good at manipulating

objects—Clive was a lot better—the tools in his left paw allowed him to grasp the cassettes and slide them out.

"Now put the new ones in their place. Be sure that the sides with the arrows go in first."

Edward wasn't sure that he had sufficient Brain to do this correctly, but the cassettes would only go in the way they were supposed to, just like with the Sinclairs' music system. As soon as he pushed the first in, the letters above the panel stopped flickering. Edward was so cheered by this that he began to sing.

Ever floated in a cavity
With a bear that lacks gravity?
You bounce, willy-nilly—
It's really rather silly!

"Bear, are you all right?" the voice in the pendant demanded.

"I am very well, thank you," said Edward. "When I am happy, I sing a song."

"You're sure you're not malfunctioning?" The man began to ask him another math question, but as soon as Edward pushed the second cassette into place, he stopped abruptly. After a second he came back, his voice sounding different. "It seems to have worked!" he cried. In the background Edward could faintly hear cheering.

"That's good," Edward said. "What would you like me to do now?"

"Eh?" The man sounded distracted. "Come on back. Perhaps you'll be good for something else."

Edward felt like another song, but he wasn't sure it

was allowed. He climbed back down to the floor and began retracing his steps, humming softly.

As soon as he turned the corner he saw another body. It was floating upside down in the dimly lit corridor, hair waving like fronds in the faint air currents. Edward was sure that it was moving, and not just drifting: every few seconds it would flex its legs slightly, as though in pain.

"Hello, are you all right?"

The person didn't turn, but the legs abruptly stopped moving. Edward marched over to the body and looked up at it. An old man's face, nose and mouth covered by an oxygen mask, hung upside down half a meter from his own.

His eyes, half-open, slowly focused on Edward, then widened. *"¡Madre de Dios!"* the man muttered, voice muffled by the mask.

"Are you all right?" Edward asked him. "It's very cold in this room, and I don't think the air is good."

The old man reached out and brushed his fingers against Edward's face. Edward offered his friendliest expression, but the man snatched his hand back, as though the touch had startled him. *"¿Está un angel?"* he asked wonderingly.

"I think you need help," Edward decided. He lowered his chin to his chest and addressed the pendant. "Hallo, Voice. Can you hear me?"

The pendant offered no response. Edward looked back apologetically toward the injured man, who had closed his eyes. "I'll get help," he told him.

Edward marched down the hallway to the door,

which had slid shut once he had squeezed through. He clambered up to the manual switch and depressed it, but the door failed to open. "Bother," said Edward. Red lights were flashing beside the panel, and he was not particularly surprised when he failed to push the door open even a centimeter.

The air pressure was lower than when he first came through, which Edward knew was a very bad thing. Emergency routines activated in his consciousness, and Edward broadcast a radio distress signal through a built-in transmitter he didn't remember having. He wasn't surprised when he received no response—an emergency might mean no radios working—and set out down the hall once more.

"I'm going to get help," he told the unmoving figure. He toddled back past the service module and stopped at a telephone, which didn't work. This didn't surprise him, either. Continuing down a series of passageways, Edward at last encountered a panel set in the wall, above which shone the letters EMERGENCY AIRLOCK in warning red.

"This is going to be rather difficult," he remarked as he tapped the keys to open the panel. Ordinarily an alarm would sound at this point, but since the emergency was already in progress, it apparently wasn't necessary. Edward climbed through the door into an open space beyond, about the size of a small closet lying on its side. It wouldn't be very big for a person, but Edward fit comfortably.

"This is the hard part," he said. He tapped a pair of keys to shut the door behind him, leaving him in total darkness save for the glow of the control pad. Edward didn't question how he knew the airlock procedures; the emergency had triggered special subroutines within his brain, which he followed without wondering. He even knew he should magnetize his paw pads, so he wouldn't be blown from the chamber when the outer door opened.

With a tap of his paw, the door at the far end of the chamber slid open. An enormous blast of wind shrieked past him, dying away to silence in less than a second. Twinkling sparks danced about him: water vapor that had frozen instantly when the air rushed out of the chamber.

Starlight shone through the open hatch. Edward walked to it and looked out at the starry night beyond. Climbing awkwardly, he stepped out of the airlock and onto the metal hull outside.

Although Edward did not need to breathe, he couldn't sing, or even hum, in a vacuum. More important, however, he couldn't function for long at extremely low temperatures, and his sensors told him that it was colder here than it ever got on Earth. He decided he had better get moving.

There was no sound in the vacuum of space, but Edward could feel the tap of his foot pads against the hull. He wondered whether anyone was on the other side, wondering who it was walking about outside. Then he remembered that this entire sector was closed off, and he would have to walk a long way to get past it. In any event, there were more important things to worry about.

Edward turned slowly, surveying the landscape

around him. The hull was almost perfectly smooth, with only an occasional hatchway or instrument assembly breaking its featureless surface. It was like standing on a tiny world, one with the horizon only a few dozen yards away.

He couldn't see what he was looking for, however, so he picked a direction and began walking.

Almost immediately he saw something that didn't look right. About a dozen yards away, the hull's gentle curve suddenly buckled, like a smooth bedsheet kicked into disorder by a restless sleeper. Edward took a few steps closer, and saw the rumpled area break into torn and twisted metal, as though something big had smashed into the hull. *Uh-oh,* he thought, but couldn't say.

Nothing suggested what exactly had happened, but Edward knew that wasn't important right now. He could see, just beyond the horizon, the tip of something protruding into space. He began to walk faster.

It took over a minute before he got close enough to confirm that the object was an antenna, and by then his feet were beginning to feel stiff. This, Edward knew, was bad news. He activated his radio transmitter and turned to face the antenna.

Hallo! he sent. *Can you hear me?* It wasn't much like talking, but he found it quite easy. Edward waited for several seconds, then shifted to a different frequency and tried again. *Hallo! Anybody there?*

He was on his fifth try when part of the antenna assembly suddenly swiveled like a tiny weather vane and aimed itself at him. *¿Quién habla? ¿Dónde está usted?*

Oh, bother, thought Edward.

He sent another message. *Can you understand me?*

There is somebody hurt in Corridor Sixty-seven. Please send help right aw—

Suddenly the hull underneath shuddered violently, as though an earthquake had rumbled up from the rooms beneath. Had Edward not kept his pads magnetized, he would have been flung into space.

Pardon me, he sent when he got his balance back. *Please send help right away!*

A light was growing on the horizon to his left, and Edward turned to look at it. As he watched, a large blue planet, three-quarters full and swirling with fleecy white clouds, rose above the metal hull and began to climb the starry sky. Edward stared in wonder. The sight tickled at the edge of his consciousness, stirring drowsing memories.

Suddenly, he knew what he was seeing. That was the Earth, and he was on a space habitat that circled high above it! How had his memories grown so muddy? And what had happened to Clive and his family?

Edward could not think longer on these matters, because the antenna transmitter abruptly spoke. *Hello, who is out there? It is unsafe to be on the hull surface at this time.*

There is somebody hurt in Corridor Sixty-seven, he repeated patiently. *I tried to come back, but the doorway is sealed.*

Someone's alive in there? There was a silence, and then a second person spoke. Even through the staticky transmission, Edward recognized the voice of the man with the smudged forehead.

Bear, is that you? The voice was openly incredulous. *How did you get out there?*

I used the airlock, Edward replied modestly.

There was a pause, and then the man spoke: *Okay, we're sending someone to check. Now you get back in. We can use you.*

Edward took a step, then stopped. *I'm afraid I can't,* he sent. He felt slightly embarrassed. *The low temperature has inactivated my servomotors.*

Eduardo, we're shifting the habitat's course, and you don't want to be out there much longer. Get in if you can, amigo.

Oh, bother, Edward tried to say. He would not have been able to speak, however, even if there had been air to speak in, for there was something wrong with his jaws. The tiny heating coil inside his tummy glowed like a furnace, but its energies fled into the chill of space. Edward felt a warning message arrive from his diagnostic program, telling him that the extreme cold was beginning to interfere with his cognitive functions.

I think we should go inside, Clive, he transmitted. *It's awfully cold out here.*

Edward tried to turn, but only the upper part of his body moved. He demagnetized one pad as he began to lift it, and at that moment the hull leapt beneath him.

Suddenly Edward was flying through space, tumbling over and over as the habitat receded from him. Stars whirled before his eyes, and every few seconds the Earth would sweep past, and then the habitat—how small it looked!—and then the Earth again. Edward had the feeling that he had done something very wrong, and that the adults would be awfully cross with him.

I'm glad you got inside, Clive, he thought confusedly.

It's quite cold out here. I must really be a Bear of Very Little . . .

His radio transmitter still worked, but no antenna monitored the fading message as he pinwheeled across the heavens. Within minutes he was lost from sight, a little bear in the big dark sky.

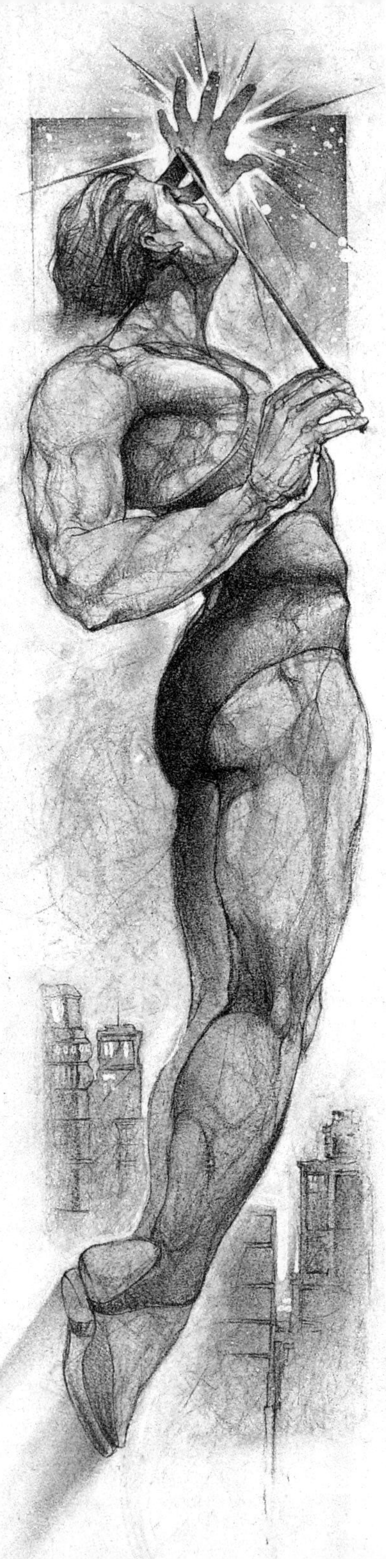

WILL SHETTERLY

SECRET IDENTITY

L.A. Academy's nickname is Hero High. Nearly half the kids, Earthers and Celestials both, have gotten their parents' permission to get their masker cards so they can legally wear strange costumes and run around looking for chances to do good in the hope of becoming famous.

Everyone assumed I'd had my card for years. Wasn't I the son of the great Galaxian? The Vampire's kid had become the

Vampire II; everyone assumed I'd be Galaxian II or Kid Galaxian or something that equally clearly announced my heritage. When I flew down the halls, people were as likely to call me Galaxian as Alec. I never bothered to correct them. The only reason I hadn't visited the Department of Masquerader Registration to make it official was that there was no rush. No one else would claim my father's masker name.

I was on my way to Latin when Steeljack called, "Hey, faggot! Yeah, you!" I winced, but I didn't look. He wasn't talking to me. To Steeljack, I was Galaxian, Jr., one of the most powerful gamma-level Celestials on the planet. He was a beta-level bully who liked tormenting alphas and Earthers.

Jason Zi'Garis answered, "Oh, S.J., you don't even have to ask. Of *course* I'll go to the prom with you." I stopped and looked then, just like everyone else within fifty feet. Half the kids laughed. Half just stared, fearing what would happen next. I was in the second group.

Those who were laughing had good reason. To Earthers and most Celestials, Jason ought to have been scary. He stood eight feet tall. His shoulders were nearly four feet wide. His grandfather had masked in the 1950s as the Big Boss Man. At sixteen, Jason was already larger and stronger than his grandfather had ever been.

But Jason was always clowning around. He'd dance down the halls like Fred Astaire when everyone else was rushing businesslike to their next class. He'd take outrageous parts in school plays and wear his costumes to class. Now, with Steeljack furious at him, Jason was affecting a high voice and a swish walk. No one could stay afraid of him.

And no one should have been afraid of Steeljack. He was a skinny kid, two-thirds Jason's height and one-fourth Jason's weight. His real name was Larry Si'Valy, but he only answered to his masker ID. He was dressed, as usual, in his registered costume, which looked a lot like a Nazi Stormtrooper's uniform.

That costume heightened their differences. Though Jason was dressed inconspicuously (for an eight-foot kid) in jeans, running shoes, and a varsity jacket, he was wearing a black T-shirt with a pink triangle across his chest. He had just registered at the DMR as the Pink Puma.

It had made the morning news in a big way. There'd always been jokes and rumors about maskers, ever since Dad showed up in tights and a cape in 1938. An Earther woman claimed to have been the Star Woman's lover, but the Star Woman was killed when the Russians invaded Hungary in '56. Though a TV movie called *Her(o)love* had been made, no one knew if that affair had really happened. Mr. Sandman had confirmed the rumors about himself when he wrote *Out of the Closet and Off with the Mask,* but Mr. Sandman was an Earther masker. Jason was the first Celestial to publicly identify himself as gay.

I looked up and down the hall for teachers and didn't see any. Steeljack had probably checked before he yelled at Jason.

"Pink Puma." Steeljack sneered. "More like, Pink Pansy."

"Ooh, wish I'd thought of that." Jason smiled as he started to walk around Steeljack. "I'll tell everyone you're the man to ask for gay masker names."

More kids laughed. I didn't. Jason was an alpha whose physical strength strained the limits of human possibility. He could take care of himself in most circumstances. But Steeljack's beta-class ability had nothing to do with human possibility. He was a metamorph whose favorite shape was that of a metal-skinned kid with razors for fingertips.

Chris Naiy was down the hall, flirting with Wanda Chan. They both got quiet when Steeljack stepped closer to Jason. Chris and Wanda glanced at me. I looked away fast.

Steeljack said, "You're pathetic, Pink Pooftah. You're disgracing Celestials, and you're disgracing maskers. You make us look like a joke."

"No way, S.J," said Jason. "You're a self-made man."

Someone snickered. As Steeljack figured it out, his skin became chrome. Someone screamed. Steeljack's fist was flashing toward Jason's head, and Jason was bringing his arm up in a block as he backed away. We all knew Jason's flesh couldn't deflect Steeljack's metal blow.

Then Chris was standing behind Steeljack. A streak the brown of Chris's skin and the red of his jacket and the yellow of his jeans seemed to hang in the hall, from the place he had been to the place he stood now. His hands were on Steeljack's shoulders, and Steeljack had been wrenched sideways. His punch ended in the air several feet away from Jason.

Chris released Steeljack, letting him lurch forward, off balance. Steeljack spun and glared. Six-inch spikes sprang from his knuckles. Then he saw what had happened. Chris was a gamma who could timeslip, making the world seem to slow down around him. Chris couldn't directly hurt Steeljack in his metal form, but Steeljack could never hope to touch Chris. It was worse than a stalemate.

In fifth grade, an older kid on a bicycle had called Chris a nigger. An instant later, the older kid was still where he had been, but his bike and his clothes were up in a tree, and the kid was covered from head to toe with chocolate syrup. The kid landed on his butt, then took off running. Everyone had called him Sundae for the next three years.

Steeljack shrugged, shifting from metal to flesh. "Hey, I wasn't really going to hit him."

Chris nodded and began to turn away.

"Besides," said Steeljack, "my complaint's with Fagman, not you."

"Yeah, Chris," said Chiller, a cryokinetic beta whose skin frosted over whenever he got excited. Right now, his hands and his face were blue with a sheen of ice. "Is widdle Jasey-wacey your boyfriend?"

Chris stared at Chiller as if that was the lamest thing he had ever heard. Then he put his arm around Jason's waist. "Why, yes, he is, and I don't care how jealous you get, you silly-chilly dude."

The crowd laughed as Chris and Jason made kissy faces. The crowd laughed more when Wanda sniffed loudly and said, "Oh, Jason, he'll break your heart like he broke mine, that shameless hussy!"

Steeljack flexed his hands. Metal razors rang like chimes. A red-headed girl smiled and called, "Hey, Larry, quit showing off." Blue-hot jets of flame appeared from her fingertips. "Skykids need to be careful. Someone might get hurt *accidentally.*"

Steeljack frowned. "Yeah, right." The razors became skin again.

The bell sounded then, and we all scrambled for our classes. Steeljack and Chiller headed one way, Wanda and the redhead ran another, Jason cartwheeled down the hall toward his room, and Chris and I raced to ours. I flew, but when I arrived, Chris was sitting comfortably in his seat. "What took you?"

I grinned, then lost the grin when Wanda whispered, "Chris wants to know why you didn't do anything. Don't you like Jase?" She was in a room two floors away, but when telepaths whisper in class, they can whisper in any class they want to.

I said, "He shouldn't have gone public if he wasn't ready for the consequences."

"You would've just watched? Steeljerk could've killed—"

"It's none of your business, Wanda."

"Well, gee, sorry I asked." Her mind left mine before I could say anything more.

After school, I flew to Geneva. Dad was getting an award from the U.N. for helping with the Balkan crisis. He wanted me to be there to be seen as the heir apparent. I smiled when I was expected to. Mostly, I was ignored. It was boring, but it was fast, and when it was done, Dad and I sprang into the air for that final photo op of Galaxian and son returning to the City of Angels.

We usually flew without talking. The best times with Dad were when we didn't need to speak. I enjoy flying, the wind whipping at my hair and my clothes, the Earth rolling beneath me. In the sky, I feel sorry for teleporters. Sure, sometimes you wish you could hop instantly from one place to another, but traveling is often better than arriving.

My thoughts were interrupted as we began to decelerate over New York. Dad flew close to say, "Earth people seem inconsequential from here, but they're not."

I glanced at him.

He said, "Never forget that, based on the genetic evidence, they're our ancestors. It doesn't matter whether an Empyrean scout ship picked up a few of them and bred us from those samples, or whether Earth's a lost Empyrean colony that never had enough enhanced stock to breed true. We have obligations to Earthers. At least as many as we have to chimpanzees. Probably more."

I shook my head. "You're such an alien, Dad."

He laughed. "So are you."

"I was born here."

"That doesn't make you one of *them.*" We flew on. Then he said, "My greatest regret is that I cannot show you the beauty of deep space."

I shrugged. I had flown to the Moon last summer. The excitement of being all by yourself in a near vacuum gets pretty thin after a few hours. I had finished the trip because I had told my friends I was going, but it had been the most boring week of my life.

On Earth, I've flown among the Andes with condors for company. I've raced tornadoes, then rested at their hearts. I've dived into storm clouds and danced with lightning.

And I've plunged into the sea to play tag with dolphins. I've watched volcanoes erupt from the ocean floor. I've hunted for human history in the forms of sunken ships and sunken cities.

And I've flown among the trees of the rain forests and invited monkeys to leap onto my back. I've followed bats into caves where no climber could ever go and accompanied sightless fish up subterranean rivers that no one but me has ever seen.

Dad said, "When we build another ship, or if one comes for us, you'll see the galaxy and know that splendor, son. The dance of the stars is slow and stately. You cannot imagine that perfection."

"No," I agreed.

I suppose I expected him to hear my sarcasm. He glanced at me. "I try to be true to myself, Alec. You must do the same."

Somewhere over the plains of the Midwest, I said, "You want me to be true to myself by becoming someone I'm not."

His sigh was carried off by the wind. "You have a responsibility to your people. That responsibility is part of who you are. I became Galaxian for many reasons. Only one was to silence the rumors that Commie-Nazi-mutant demons from outer space were hiding among ordinary Americans. There's still a need to assure Earthers that we only want to live here in peace."

I said, "Three thousand, four hundred, and eighty-one."

"What?"

"That's how many times you've told me Celestials

need a wholesome, all-American, apple pie–eating representative, or we'll be feared and persecuted."

He smiled. "I think you placed the decimal too far to the right, but I take your point." I didn't smile. He said, "Being Galaxian is a chance to help Celestials and Earthers both. You'd be surprised how good that makes you feel."

"Yeah. You're a saint, Dad."

I figured I had made another point, though it didn't make me happy. He said, "Fair enough. I enjoy the fame and glory, too. Too much, sometimes. If I'd indulged in fewer of the opportunities that came my way—"

I wondered if he would mention Mom or the affairs or the divorce, but he didn't. Somewhere over the Rockies, I said, "A Celestial I know got his masker card and announced he was gay."

Dad winced. "I heard. I wish he hadn't."

"Why?"

"During the Second World War, the U.S. confined thousands of Japanese-Americans in camps. There was also a camp for Celestials. Super-powered homosexuals would be some Earthers' greatest nightmare."

"The kid I know says if you hide, you're admitting you have something to feel guilty about."

Dad looked at me. "We want to live in peace on this planet, Alec. That's all we want. Why make trouble over things that aren't important?"

I nodded. We had reached L.A., and now we hovered high above our house.

He said, "Will you be at the Masqueraders' Ball?"

"I'm the heir of the great Galaxian. Of course I'll be there, O great Galaxian."

"We'll speak then. Remember that I love you, son."

I watched as he flew south. He had told Amnesty International that he would spend a few days hunting for political prisoners in Central America.

I whispered, "Bastard." If he was listening, he did not look back.

After dinner—a cheese sandwich I made at home—I flew to Wilshire Boulevard, landed in an alley, and walked to our favorite café. No one noticed me until I sat across from a Celestial whose size could not be hidden by custom-made street clothes. Then there were the usual whispers as people wondered if I was also a masker or a movie star or someone famous. After all, I was meeting with the Celestial whose face had been on all the news shows. The wondering about us died quickly, and no one came to ask for autographs.

Jason said, "I'm glad you came."

I said, "I had to."

The waiter approached. Jason told her, "The usual." She smiled and left.

I said, "If Steeljerk'd hit you, I would've killed him."

He laughed. "I know that."

The waiter set a root beer in front of me and a cappuccino in front of Jason, telling him, "It'll stunt your growth."

He said, "Promises, promises."

The waiter grinned and left. I said, "She must think we're mighty cute together."

"And why not? We are."

"Well." I blushed. "Look—"

"You don't have to explain."

"It's—Dad would think I'd betrayed our people."

Jason shook his head. "He'd think you'd betrayed his people. He'd be right."

"Gee, thanks. That's sure comforting." I stared at the foam of my root beer.

Jason did his John Wayne. "A man's got to do what a man's got to do." Then he added, "It doesn't change how we feel about each other."

"I'm worried about you going on patrol. You'll be a target—"

He nodded. "A mighty big target. Gaybashers look for easy prey."

"I don't like it."

"So tag along. My route hits the parks and the gay neighborhoods. It'll be a walking date."

I shook my head and couldn't look at his face.

He laughed. "Your dad would love the headlines. 'Galaxian's Son Cruises Homosexual Hangouts.' "

I shrugged.

Jason's voice shifted suddenly. He said, " 'Gee, Jase, why don't we talk about other things?' 'Sure, Alec; what do you want to talk about?' 'How about your beautiful eyes, Jase, you great big gorgeous hunk of a man, you?' "

I wanted to say he did a lousy imitation of me, but I heard myself laugh instead. We talked about school and friends and how the world should be changed. Then he went on patrol, and I flew back to do some homework. The eleven o'clock news showed him strolling through the streets in costume while people cheered. An ancient Hispanic woman said she thought he was wonderful. A guy who looked like he had an ulcer said he thought Jason was disgusting. A younger guy said,

"White maskers, black maskers, human maskers, skyguy maskers, straight maskers, gay maskers. They're all egomaniacs in tights. Who cares?" That's one form of acceptance.

I wanted to be with Jason. Then I thought about Dad and the harrassment I'd get at school, and I decided I'd done the right thing.

I woke on the sofa. Something needed my attention. I had the phone to my ear before I understood what was happening. Jason's mom said, "Alec? Pamela Zi'Garis." Her voice was quietly formal, which seemed odd; I'd had dinner at their house, and she'd been as loud and happy as her son. "Jason asked me to call. First, you should know that he's going to be all right, and second—" She inhaled suddenly, then said, "He'd like to see you. Visiting hours—"

"Where is he?" I asked.

"Kennedy Clinic, Room Seven-thirteen. Visiting hours—"

"Thanks." I hung up the phone. Three minutes later, I set my bare feet onto the hospital roof near the helicopter landing pad, found an open door, flew down the stairwell to the seventh floor, scanned the hallway for watchers, and flew into Jason's room.

He was asleep, breathing raggedly. Two beds had been pushed together to hold him. Two sheets had been draped over him. In the dim light, his skin was blue. His head was bandaged. One leg and one arm were in casts.

About an hour before dawn, a nurse looked in. "Who're—"

I put my finger to my lips, then followed her into the hall. "Did they catch them?"

"Catch who?"

"Whoever did this. Were they caught?"

"They usually aren't. How'd you get in?"

"I flew."

She frowned, studied my face, then nodded. "He'll be fine. Go home, get some sleep, come back after school, okay? That's when visiting hours officially begin."

"Can you tell me what happened?"

"I can tell you what the clues suggest, but they don't make sense."

"Okay."

"Someone hit him in the face with a ball of slush that froze over his eyes. Then someone took a metal club and beat him until he collapsed."

I nodded, thanked her, and flew away.

Steeljack and Chiller sauntered into the schoolyard about ten minutes before the first bell. They quit sauntering when I landed on the sidewalk in front of them. Surprise touched their faces for only an instant, but I could hear their hearts continue to race like drums in a bad jungle movie. Kids passing by looked at us, then gave us plenty of room. I said, "Why'd you do it?"

"Do what?" said Chiller.

"Come on," Steeljack told him. "Young Galaxian thinks we did something we didn't."

"Yes, you did." Wanda's telepathic whisper vibrated in all of our skulls. She stepped out onto the front steps so Steeljack and Chiller could see her.

Chiller's hand began to frost over. "Says who?"

"Says you," said Wanda. "Loud and clear."

"Forget it," said Steeljack. "Mind reading's not admissible in court."

"Who said anything about court?" Chris appeared beside me. For an instant, a shimmer of brown and blue ran up the sidewalk to show where he'd been, then it dissipated.

Steeljack stepped backward. "Oh, yeah, right. Gang up on us."

I said, "You set a fine example." Then I said, "Relax. Jase won't press charges. He didn't see anyone's face. He didn't hear anyone's voice. He couldn't make anything stick. It worked just like you planned."

Steeljack and Chiller glanced at each other. Steeljack smiled a little, and the soundtrack of their heartbeats slowed.

I said, "Legal charges aren't Jase's style. He says if you'll get counseling, he'll forget the whole thing."

"Dream on." A cloud of cold air shot from Chiller's throat as he laughed.

Chris said, "Be kind of rough, coming to school and never knowing whether your clothes were going to disappear at any instant. Whether you might suddenly have the worst haircut you'd ever seen. Whether you might find yourself wearing a clown nose or a pair of diapers."

Chiller stared. "You wouldn't."

Steeljack said, "Wouldn't dare." His hand became a spiked ball on a steel chain that he began to whirl at his side. "If you declare war, someone's going to get hurt."

"You already declared war," I said. "Someone's already gotten hurt. But you're right that if we continue like this, things'll only get worse."

Steeljack grinned.

I said, "So maybe I should fly you to the top of Kilimanjaro or Mount Everest. Got a preference?"

Steeljack sneered. "I'd get back. One way or another."

"Yeah," I said. "So maybe I should drop you in the middle of the ocean."

"Hah," said Steeljack. His hand became a knife that he pointed at me. I stared at it. He returned his hand to flesh, but continued to point at me. "You pacifist pussies don't scare me."

"Pacifist pussies," Chiller repeated with pleased respect.

"It's a problem," I admitted. "Wanda?"

"Meow." She strolled down the steps, waving to Chiller and Steeljack like a cat stretching its claws. "People like you must've gone through some horrible things to turn out like you did."

Steeljack touched his chest with both hands. "Oh, no. Poor little misunderstood me." He and Chiller snickered. Steeljack said, "Keep your pity."

"Pity? Huh-uh." Wanda smiled. "A telepath following you around, digging into your thoughts, could learn a lot. Things that everyone would know. Things that'd be waiting around school for you, written on the blackboards and in the washrooms. Think about it."

Chiller swallowed. "That's blackmail."

Chris nodded. "Give the man a prize."

Steeljack said, "I thought telepaths could only read surface thoughts."

Wanda smiled. "Do you really want to find out?"

Steeljack looked at each of us. After a moment, he shook his head.

Chris said, "By this afternoon, we want to hear that you've met with a counselor and confessed. Got it?"

Chiller shivered. Steeljack said quietly, "Okay." They began to walk by.

I said, "Oh, something you should know." I pulled a masker ID out of my jacket pocket. "Guess who registered today?" I held the card out so they could see my photo, my name and address, and the name typed in as my masquerader identity. Steeljack and Chiller looked at it, then at me, and walked away shaking their heads.

Chris said, "You think therapy will do them any good?"

Wanda stared at him. "Who cares? They'll *hate* it."

Jason grinned when he saw me hovering outside his hospital window, pressing my masker card against the glass. In my skull, I heard Wanda's whisper. "He says he heard it on the radio, Gaylaxian. You didn't need to skip school to tell him."

"That's not why I skipped school."

I stayed by the window. Wanda said, "I wish I could give you two some privacy. But then you couldn't communicate."

I said, "Yes, we can." I blew Jason a kiss, and then I did a triple back-flip in the air. I didn't need to hear his laugh to know how it sounded.

DAVE TROWBRIDGE

SURAKI

Taj was soaring. Free of the chains of gravity inside a bubble of stone high above the planet Sundara, he had just reached the peak of his climb when a small voice spoke in his ear.

"Time's up."

Taj groaned. He'd almost forgotten that the only real things he was experiencing were his sport-flying wings and the effort of using them. The rest was a cleverly programmed fiction in a firmly planet-bound simulator.

The color slowly began to fade out of the vine-tangled cliffs around him as the shutdown sequence began. Taj wheeled about and began a steep dive toward a grassy sphere far below, at the center of the orbital flight resort being reproduced by the simulator. At the last possible moment he opened his wings and, with a final burst of energy that he felt deep in his chest, swooped upward and firmly planted his feet. Then he ran his thumbs across his fingertips, flexing the control gloves in the shutdown sequence, and relaxed as his wings began to pull away from his arms and legs and fold into a compact bundle.

A mild dizziness washed through Taj as the gravity slowly increased back to normal. Suddenly the scene around him wavered, as though seen through running water, and dissolved into the gray dyplast interior of the simulator, leaving him standing on a small platform a bare meter off the scuffed deck of the sim. He could hear the dull whine of the wind generators subsiding. Behind him, the door clanked open.

"So, Taj, you ready for WingWorld?"

Taj twisted around, his collapsing wings still an awkward bundle on his back and legs, as Mari's silvery voice echoed in the huge room. She smiled at him, her dark eyes sparkling.

"Huh?" Taj felt his face burn; Mari had replaced the dour old man who used to run the sim only a week ago, and he still felt tongue tangled at the sight of her. It didn't help that she treated him like a kid brother. "No, I'm going to Talajara. Didn't Flugel tell you? Gee-Em invited me."

Mari's eyes widened. "The Talajara nuller? You know her?"

"Gee-Em was my name-day sponsor." He waved an arm around at the sim. "And she's the one who pays for this." Emboldened by the sudden respect in Mari's face, he added, "My dad says she may even sponsor me to the Academy on Minerva."

"You're very fortunate," Mari said. Then she frowned. "But Talajara's a highdwelling."

Struck by the sudden doubt in her voice, Taj suddenly remembered that Mari herself was a highdweller, born in one of the huge cylindrical constructs in orbit around Sundara.

He shrugged, trying to project a confidence he didn't feel. "So? It's just bigger, and it rotates to make gees, instead of using a big gravitor at the center. But up at the spin axis it's low gees, just like WingWorld. Besides, the sim doesn't have any highdwelling chips; Flugel said this would teach me what I needed to know."

He swung the collapsed wing pack to the floor. "And I've been flying for five years now—this was just to get a feel for doing it in a real place, instead of a fantasy landscape."

"I can tell," she said. "Your shoulders and chest are as big as any of the fledgies' in Aramapriya, where I grew up." Mari shook her head. "But you're a downsider, and so is Flugel. He—" She broke off politely as Taj's boswell beeped. He looked down at the little datalink on his wrist and gasped.

"Gonna be late; my S'lift pod climbs in thirty minutes." He picked up his wings and ran out. Mari called out after him, but the echoes from the interior of the sim muffled her voice, and all he heard was a single word.

It sounded like "Suraki."

Somebody's name?

Taj barely made it to the transtube in time: the doors squawked a warning at him as he flung himself into the transport. As it accelerated toward the S'lift, the immense cable that reached all the way from Sundara's surface to the ring of highdwellings in orbit forty thousand kilometers above, Taj mulled over Mari's reaction, struggling with an odd knot of emotions.

"Your shoulders and chest are as big as any of the fledgies' in Aramapriya . . ." She'd said "fledgie"—a real flyer—instead of "eyaz"—someone yet to make their first flight. And the admiration in her voice had been a welcome change from his schoolmates' teasing. It was bad enough that he was from a family newly raised to the Douloi aristocracy. What really set him apart were the wide shoulders and deep chest that the intense effort of flying had given him: the very opposite of the slender physique considered fashionable. But Mari didn't mind that at all.

Then he remembered her next words.

"But you're a downsider . . ." Her tone then had definitely *not* been admiring. His stomach twisted—how would people treat him up on Talajara? One reason he was looking forward to his visit to one of the highdwellings was that there a flyer was not a freak. But was being a downsider up there even worse than being a flyer down below?

When he got to the terminal, Taj grabbed his wing pack and ran to the waiting lift, which deposited him outside the towering S'lift pod just before its doors hissed shut. The steward's voice was already droning through the usual emergency procedures as he found his seat.

". . . accelerating at one-tenth gee for approximately forty minutes, during which time you will feel a bit heavier than normal . . ."

The pod lifted with an almost imperceptible shudder, climbing so slowly that it was almost a minute before the roof of the terminal finally cut off the sight of the crowded concourse.

But he hardly noticed. Would Gee-Em, his mysterious benefactor, really sponsor him to the Naval Academy on far-off Minerva, halfway across the Thousand Suns?

He'd never met Gee-Em, or not that he could remember, but he knew that her attendance at his name-day ritual a month after his birth had caused a sensation. Nullers—those rare humans able to adapt to permanent life in the weightlessness of null-gee—almost never descended to the surface of a planet. The centuries-long lifespan bestowed by null-gee—Gee-Em herself was over 350 years old—was too precious to risk: if the geebubble that kept them weightless failed, it would mean a swift and agonizing death in the crushing grip of planetary gravity.

Taj had no idea why she'd picked him out, alone of all her descendants in his generation. Her trust fund had financed his education and his flying, and now she had summoned him without explanation to her home up in Talajara.

The thought reminded him of her invitation, written in spidery handwriting on stiff, creamy paper, after the fashion favored by the Douloi for intimate communications.

"*. . . and I suggest that you view the orientation vid with great care on the way up, for life on a highdwelling is far different from what you have known.*"

At his touch a viewscreen extruded from the seat back in front of him. He selected the orientation and settled back to watch. At first the images of the highdwelling held his attention. It was a vast cylinder spinning about its long axis to create gravity. People lived on the inner surface in elegant buildings set amongst trees and greenery, and Taj found the idea of an inside-out world both beautiful and strange. But soon he was distracted by the breathtaking panorama out the viewport. The horizon curved off below a deep violet sky as the cloud-swirled surface of Sundara fell swiftly away.

". . . The fact that gravity on a highdwelling is furnished by rotation rather than mass or a gravitor has some interesting consequences. For instance, 'light' objects actually fall faster than 'heavy' ones."

Startled, Taj looked back at the screen, where a cartoon figure tossed a huge lump of orange foam off a platform with a flick of its wrists, then labored mightily to roll a small metal sphere off the edge after it.

"If you push equal masses of dyplast foam and lead away from the spin axis, where they are both weightless, the foam falls faster—that is, it falls along a shorter path and thus reaches the inner surface far sooner than the lead." On the screen, the foam fell faster and faster as it descended, while the lead ball seemed to float lazily through the air.

"This is because the air within the highdwelling, which is, of course, rotating along with everything else, easily accelerates the lighter foam up to the rate of rotation so that it is immediately subject to spin-gravity. The heavier lead, on the other hand, is almost unaffected by the rotational wind, so it isn't subject to the highdwelling's spin-gravity. It falls in a long spiral and hits the surface long after the lighter foam.

"The difference is further exaggerated by the fact that the farther an object is from the spin axis—the lower it is—the heavier it gets, and the change with altitude is much greater than on a planet or in a gravitor-equipped habitat. This explains why the myth of Icarus, so familiar to downsiders, is—"

Taj grimaced and tabbed the vid off. That was the nickname the other students had stuck him with—Icky. It was a stupid story, anyway—a boy flying on wings made of wax and feathers that melted from the sun's heat when he flew too high. Everyone knew you couldn't fly like that on a planet—people were too heavy.

"This mudfoot vid is boring," said a boy behind him.

"It's eight hours to the Node," replied a girl, whose voice sent a shiver of delight through Taj and pulled him out of his thoughts. "What do you want to do?"

"Let's go up to the salon and see what kind of games they've got."

As they passed, she glanced at Taj and smiled briefly, and he saw that she was, if possible, even prettier than her voice: long, straight dark hair, high cheekbones, and a perfect dark olive high-caste complexion.

Taj hesitated. They were obviously highdwellers—the reference to the vid as "mudfoot" in origin proved that. Even more daunting, their singsong voices identified them as High Douloi. Social convention was strict: they would have to make the first move toward acquaintance. Any overture on his part would doubtless be greeted with the freezing formality he'd encountered all too often from his schoolmates.

But the boy with her seemed to have a flyer's build, so evidently downsider Douloi fashions didn't hold in orbit. And Taj remembered how she'd smiled at him—with more than just her mouth, he thought.

The sound of laughter drifting down from the salon, mixed with the faint blaring of a simgame, decided him. He stood up, hesitated a moment, then took his wing pack with him.

His heart pounding, Taj climbed the stairs, emerging into a luxuriously carpeted cabin crowded with young people. An especially animated knot of them was gathered around a low console, across which a tall boy and a girl with a stiff shock of bright blue hair faced each other, tapping frantically at the keypads to a mixture of musical and explosive noises. It sounded comfortably familiar.

Taj awkwardly pushed his way to the front of the crowd, impeded by his wing pack, and verified his suspicion: They were playing Acheront, a vidgame based on the famous space battle that had ended the war with Dol'jhar. He'd trained many times in the official Academy sim of that battle.

He watched with growing impatience as the boy conning the frigate *Tirane* maneuvered it timidly from asteroid to asteroid, creeping up on the crippled Dol'jharian flagship. In the real battle, Ensign Margot

O'Reilly Ng had boldly charged the *Blood of Dol* and captured the avatar while the ship's ruptors were off line.

But the boy's cautious play earned him a very different reward: The other player crowed with triumph as her battlecruiser's ruptors suddenly powered up and discharged. Vicious pulses of gravitational energy tore into the little frigate, disintegrating it in a blare of light.

Taj groaned in disgust. The loser looked up; he was the pretty girl's companion. In fact, she was standing right behind him.

"You think you could do better?" he asked, his singsong accent diminished by the anger in his voice.

Taj thought he saw a glimmer of encouragement in the girl's eyes. Emboldened, he stepped up to the console.

"Sure," he replied.

The blue-haired girl yielded her seat with a sidelong glance.

Across the simgame console the loser eyed Taj's wing pack. "Where are you from?" he asked as he reset the game, his High Douloi accent returning.

"Vishnara."

"A downsider. What're you doing with a wing pack?"

"I'm going up to Talajara to fly."

"We're from Talajara," said the girl. "I'm Amavira." She touched the shoulder of the boy in front of her. "This is my brother, Naramutro."

"Tajarivani," Taj said in response. Then, not allowing time for a possible snub, he added a note of informality: "Taj."

She smiled. "Ama."

Taj abruptly felt very light. He smiled back.

But Naramutro just nodded, not offering a nickname, and motioned at the simgame console. "Your choice."

A thrill ran through Taj. Naramutro was treating this like a formal duel.

He glanced past his opponent, out the viewport. The sky was black now as the S'lift pod climbed toward space. Above, the bright arch of the ring of highdwellings about the planet formed a vivid stroke of light over the curve of Sundara's horizon.

Taj suddenly realized that the S'lift was not only carrying him into orbit, it was also carrying him away from his old identity. Up here no one knew him; he didn't have to be "Icky" anymore.

With a boldness he'd formerly reserved for the battlesims he replied, "Random."

Naramutro's lips tightened as a whispered current of excitement ran through the others. The girl who'd just beaten Naramutro suppressed a laugh. Taj had thrown away his advantage by letting the simgame choose any of the millions of scenarios stored in its memory. In effect, he'd just announced that he could beat Naramutro at any game.

And he proved it. The simgame windowed up a duel between battlecruisers in a dense asteroid belt. Within fifteen minutes Taj had maneuvered behind Naramutro's cruiser and delivered a crippling blow to his opponent's radiants, a notable weak spot in those otherwise almost invulnerable ships. Before Taj could launch a second hypermissile to finish him off, Naramutro slapped the CONCEDE tab and sat back, his face dark with anger.

"You worked the sims pretty hard downside, didn't you?" The High Douloi's voice was almost a snarl. Before Taj could reply the other boy went on. "I suppose that's how you learned to fly, too."

"Sort of hard to fly downside, otherwise," said the girl with the shock of blue hair. She grinned at Taj.

Naramutro stood up. "It takes more than simtime to make a fledgie from an eyaz. Not that you're likely to find out." He turned to Ama. "Come on, Ama. The air's a bit thick in here."

Taj flushed at the slighting reference to his downsider origins—the atmosphere on most of the highdwellings was thinner than Sundara's.

Ama shook her head. "You go on, Nara; I think I'll play a few games."

Naramutro stared at her for a moment, then turned and walked out, his gait stiff.

The others crowded around Taj, congratulating him on his victory and offering introductions at a speed that taxed his memory.

"You've got problems with Nara," said Elli, the blue-haired girl. "He's the cadet master of the aerie in Talajara, and he's sure to hand you the black feather."

"I've got a red feather already," said Taj.

Elli's brow knitted in doubt and Ama said, "It may not be enough; our uncle is the temenarch of Talajara."

But then her eyes widened as Taj, feeling doubtful himself, pulled his aerie pass out of a pocket and held it out on the palm of his hand. It was just a piece of red dyplast, shaped like a small feather, with an embedded datachip; but on it was inlaid a gold circle with two wings.

Elli burst into laughter. "I'd like to see Nara black-feather this one. That's Gee-Em's sigil!"

"She's my greatmother in the twelfth generation," explained Taj. "I'm visiting her on Talajara."

"Then we're cousins," said Ama. Perhaps a bit of Taj's disappointment showed, for she added—with just the hint of a wink, he was sure—"in the fourth degree. *Distant* cousins."

"What kind of wings are those?" interrupted Tulli, a Talajaran boy with a square face and stocky build.

"Jihari Apodines. They're modeled after the swifts brought by the Exiles from Lost Earth."

Ama looked at the wing pack longingly. "My parents won't let me fly sport; I have to use an old set of Creswill Diomedes. Just once I'd like to do more than just soar."

"They don't want you to lose your figure," said Elli. Taj heard a mixture of envy and challenge in her voice. He noticed for the first time that the blue-haired girl had the wide shoulders of a flyer who used highly maneuverable wings like his, in contrast to Ama's willowy frame.

Elli turned to him and squeezed his shoulder. "You've got great wings, Gee-Em's chop, and a good set of flight muscles—I'm looking forward to seeing your first real flight." She smiled. "Maybe we can fly together."

"That'd be great! Maybe we can all meet at the aerie."

Much of the rest of the journey to the Node was spent playing simgames, which he kept winning until Ama, Elli, and Tulli ganged up on him in a three-destroyer-versus-battlecruiser scenario that ended in a spectacular explosion. After that, they all talked and joked. Being the center of attention was an unfamiliar and heady sensation for Taj, so he barely noticed their impending arrival until one especially funny story made him laugh so hard he floated out of his seat. They were at the Node, the main link between Sundara and its highdwellings, and the Thousand Suns beyond.

From there it was a short shuttle flight to Talajara Highdwelling. Taj didn't see Naramutro on the little ship, but Ama merely said that her brother would probably take a different flight. Taj couldn't decipher her expression.

From the shuttle they disembarked into an enormous ring concourse that circled the inside of one of Talajara's end caps, the one his highdweller friends called the south pole. There, close to the spin axis, the gravity was about one-eighth of Sundara's, but if Taj moved slowly the sticky shoe covers he had been issued let him walk almost normally.

Taj looked around, and what he saw made him dizzy. To either side of him the floor curved up under a ceiling perhaps fifty meters high, both paralleling in miniature the curve of the habitat's sides. In the distance, before the ceiling cut off his view almost a half kilometer away, he could see the tiny figures of people hurrying about canted over at an angle of forty-five degrees to him. He knew that at every point along the concourse, spin-gravity was straight down, but he still couldn't quite shake the feeling that at any moment all of those people would suddenly come sliding down into a giant heap, with him at the bottom.

Ahead, looking down the length of Talajara through

the opening at the edge of the curved floor and ceiling of the concourse, Taj saw a huge smile-shaped slice of blue sky with strange hook-topped clouds ringing a pair of enormous glowing tubes. The tubes speared out overhead and converged in the misty distance, a blindingly bright spot of light midway along each of them. And farther out he saw what appeared to be islands hanging in the sky—or were they mountains?

His planet-bred mind couldn't make sense of the scene, which pulled him forward, his friends following silently. As he approached the edge, he realized that the concourse was nothing more than a huge balcony overlooking the interior of Talajara, with no concessions to the fears of downsiders. Only a low railing separated him from a sheer four-kilometer drop.

On the railing Taj saw a bright red sign with a chilling message:

ATTENTION TRAVELERS:
DROPPING AN OBJECT FROM HERE
IS PUNISHABLE BY DEATH!

A moment's thought told him why: the surface of Talajara was rotating at more than seven hundred kilometers per hour with respect to the spin axis, so an object of any significant weight falling from here would hit with incredible force: a kind of trash meteorite.

But then Taj forgot everything else as he got his first look at the interior of Talajara.

He stood for a long time at the railing, at the edge of a green cliff covered with vines bearing sweet-smelling flowers. The cliff dropped sheer to a cottony cloud layer that obscured the view directly below, but farther away the clouds broke up a little, revealing the distant inner surface of the highdwelling. A tapestry of villages and fields interspersed with tall buildings stretched into the hazy distance, stitched through with the bright gleaming of streams and ponds. The far end of Talajara was invisible, while to either side the land curved up into dizzying overhangs—what his eyes had first seen as mountains—that were lost in the dazzle of the diffusers overhead, the huge tubular structures stretching from pole to pole that delivered sunlight to the interior.

It was beautiful and utterly strange. Every time he looked straight ahead, it was pretty much like being in an aircar on Sundara. But then the disorienting landscape curving up on either side, with buildings jutting sideways out of huge green overarching cliffs, reminded him he was inside an enormous cylinder. He knew that to the people in those buildings, he would be the one apparently hanging sideways. Thinking about it made him dizzy all over again.

"The aerie's at the north pole," said Ama. "Where are you staying?"

As he opened his mouth to answer, his boswell buzzed with a LOCATE signal and a swift glitter in the distance arrested his attention. Between one breath and another it swooped up and resolved into an incredibly ancient human enclosed in a shimmering bubble. Taj couldn't see the machinery that kept the geebubble weightless, just a kind of spindly chair in which the nuller was seated. The geebubble hesitated momentarily in front of him before darting over the railing and into the concourse. Taj twisted to face the bubble as it abruptly stopped and hovered a few centimeters off the floor. He found himself face-to-face with his ancestor twelve generations removed.

Gee-Em's face was deeply seamed with wrinkles, her eyes a fierce bright blue, and only the long iron gray hair floating loose around her head identified her as female, so much had three and a half centuries of life withered her. Her limbs, as far as Taj could see in the enveloping folds of the garment floating around her, were incredibly thin. But her bare hands and feet were strong and sinewy, as were her wrists and ankles. A constant breeze blew from the bubble, generated by the gravitational difference between its weightless interior and the outside. The breeze smelled of roses and dust.

"Greetings, Tajarivani vlith-Ramajugandra," she said in a surprisingly strong voice. Her use of the inheritance prefix "vlith" acknowledged his position as heir. Next to him he felt Elli's sudden stare fall on him.

Taj bowed in a full formal deference, feeling awkward, a sensation intensified by the fact that Gee-Em floated at a slight angle to the floor. He found himself leaning sideways as they talked.

"You do me honor," he replied. Her meeting him here, instead of waiting for him to come to her, was an inversion of the usual etiquette.

"Not honor but necessity," she said, waving aside formality with a graceful gesture. "I'm afraid the press of business will keep me from my duties as your host, at least for a short time, so I have arranged for your lodging at the Hack."

"Oh! I . . . Thank you!"

As he spoke, Taj heard the sharp intake of breath

from his three friends. The Hack was the ultra-exclusive hotel near the Talajara aerie that catered specifically to flyers. Then, noting the direction of Gee-Em's gaze, he collected himself and introduced his suddenly shy companions.

But Gee-Em quickly put them at ease with a brief conversation with each—not like grown-ups usually did, but as if she really cared about what they said, as if they were responsible adults. Taj suddenly realized that, as old as she was, there probably wasn't all that much difference to her between people his age and adults his parents' age.

"Of course, I needn't inquire about your interests," she said to Taj with a smile that made her face even more wrinkly, if that were possible. She motioned at his wing pack. "I'm sure you're eager to put those to use—Apodines, aren't they?"

He nodded dumbly. Then her boswell chimed.

"Your pardon, greatson, but time presses," she said after a glance at her wrist. She waved toward the railing. "And the clouds are calling you."

He bowed deeply, realizing the interview was at an end; but then she squinted at him, her gaze suddenly sharp. "You watched the orientation, did you not?"

"Umm . . . yes."

"Very well. Fair winds to you, then. And to you all."

With that, her bubble spun about and darted off down the concourse, skimming over the heads of the hurrying throng until it disappeared above the curve of the ceiling.

"I wonder what it's like to fly in a geebubble," said Elli.

"She seemed a little abrupt," commented Ama.

"My dad says that nullers don't like to waste time," said Tulli. " 'Cause they've seen enough of it go by to know how valuable it is."

But Taj said nothing. What would she have said if he'd admitted he hadn't watched the whole vid? Why was it important to her?

His anxiety lasted long after his friends left, promising to meet him at the aerie the next morning. Even the astounding luxury of the Hack didn't entirely shake it. He fell asleep still wondering if he'd made a mistake.

The next morning, before dawn, a hotel aircar took him to the aerie, where he found Ama, Elli, and Tulli waiting for him. Naramutro was there as well. Taj braced himself for a confrontation as he held out the red feather given him by Gee-Em, but the other boy was carefully polite, and to Taj's surprise, he assigned him and his friends one of the best set of perches in the aerie. Not that Naramutro stiffed himself; Taj noticed that he took up a position nearby.

As they unpacked their wings the diffusers slowly kindled near the other pole. The bright spot of light relayed by the huge mirrors outside the highdwelling would move slowly along the length of the diffusers until it reached this pole and put an end to flying for the day—the heat generated wind currents too unpredictable for even the most skillful flyers. As the light in the diffusers swelled, it gradually revealed an astonishing waterfall cascading in a feathery spiral around the north pole of Talajara down to the rain forest below. A fitful breeze carried its muted thunder to their ears.

They chatted quietly while they inspected their wings. A flyer's wing sets actually had two pairs of wings, like dragonflies, plus a tail, manipulated by the legs and feet, for directional control. The first set of wings, the lift wings, didn't move, but could be tilted and trimmed to change the amount of lift generated. The other pair, the flight wings, actually propelled the flyer, whose arms and chest muscles moved them in a circular motion, cupping the air and pushing back and down. The flight angle of the wings and their quillions—dyplast feathers—were coordinated by a computer operated by the flight gloves.

Ama carefully unfolded her Diomedes, which had short flight wings and long, graceful lift wings for slow, soaring flight. Elli, it turned out, had a pair of Jihari Tiercels, designed for fast flight and dramatic dives. Tulli carefully combed the quillions on the flight wings of an old pair of Megharan Passerines before putting them on while he watched Taj spread the colorful lift wings of his Apodines. Taj felt Naramutro watching him. He smiled to show there were no hard feelings, but the other boy turned away and launched himself out into the air. His wings looked like they might be Apodines, too.

"Come on," said Tulli when they all had their wings on. "Let's go!"

Taj stood for a moment, feeling an unfamiliar vertigo as he watched his friends launch themselves out into the air, with Talajara's distant surface curving up clifflike on either side. It was so different from the simulator: most of his flying had been done over planetary landscapes that existed only in the imagination of artists, and the WingWorld bubbloid was far smaller than Talajara.

A group of kids swooped by, led by Naramutro. One of them cocked his head toward Taj and sneered, "Mudfoot."

Taj flushed, flexed his legs, and jumped. Low gee was low gee. As the strong strokes of his wings caught the cool air, the familiar excitement of flight wiped away his doubts.

At first he stayed with his friends, darting around Ama as she soared, mock dogfighting with Elli in her more maneuverable wings, and briefly playing tag with Tulli and some other kids. But, to his surprise, he found he was a better flyer than any of them.

Later, during a brief rest on his perch, he watched the flyers around Naramutro, now including Elli, play an unfamiliar version of scoopball, which he'd often practiced in the simulator. They used the standard gear: helmets with a scoop on top that was used to catch and then launch a small ball. But here there was no playing space and no goal hoops. They just tossed the ball and retrieved it in darting swoops. He couldn't figure out the point.

Tulli landed next to him, followed by Ama.

"What happens if they drop the ball?" asked Taj, remembering the sign on the concourse.

"It's got a gas cylinder in it that triggers if they lose it," said Tulli. "It balloons up and floats back up to the axis."

Suddenly Naramutro flew up and hovered in front of them. "I've been watching you," he said. "You're not too bad, for a downsider—you want to try some real flying?"

"AyKay," replied Taj, feeling a tingle of excitement in his chest.

"Be careful," whispered Ama. "They fly rough. And Nara's still angry about the simgame; he doesn't like to lose."

"I'll look out," he said, warmed by her concern.

"Just work with me," said Elli, who had flown up as Naramutro darted away. "I'll show you the moves."

At first Taj felt a little clumsy, not fully understanding the strategy of the game, but he soon caught on. The goal mostly seemed to be to swoop in and intercept the ball before another flyer could catch it; but there was an elaborate etiquette of avoidance and alliance that he slowly came to understand with Elli's help.

After a while he sensed the attitudes of the others changing. A couple of them actually cheered when he pulled off a graceful chandelle, reversing direction at the point of a stall to slip under the ball and snatch it away only inches from Elli's scoop. She laughed and fell away in a reverse loop; he launched the ball toward her, only to have it intercepted by Naramutro.

He climbed after the other boy, shadowing him closely, feeling the strain in his chest and arms as he and Naramutro zigzagged across the sky, Talajara wheeling around them. Taj could hear the other's harsh breathing and realized that he was panting just as hard.

Just then Naramutro twisted swiftly in a complex turn, falling away and behind and tossing the ball toward one of his friends. But Taj was ready. He slipped sideways, spilling air from his flight wings and twisting violently in a move that made the quillions on his wings whistle. He caught the ball just ahead of the girl's scoop and fell away as she yelled in frustration.

He heard Elli laugh. "Air too thick for you, Nara?" she crowed.

Naramutro didn't reply, and instead stooped viciously on Taj, coming far closer than he should have. But Taj didn't flinch. Instead, he spread his wings and turned to meet him. The maneuver created a whirl of wind that spoiled the other boy's lift and caused Naramutro to spiral away for a few seconds in a clumsy flutter.

Naramutro flew back toward him and hovered. "Is that how you want it, mudfoot?" Then, not waiting for an answer, he threw back his head and shouted, "Suraki!"

The cry was taken up by some of the others. "Suraki, suraki!"

"No!" shouted Elli. "You know it's forbidden!" But her voice was lost in the swelling chorus as a swirl of flyers descended around them. Taj yielded the ball to one of them, who had motioned for it. Was this what Mari had referred to in the simulator down on Sundara?

But then the girl he'd thrown the ball to tossed it down, and someone else swooped under, caught it, and then launched it farther down, toward the distant surface. Taj watched for a moment, then joined in: He caught it, then tossed it down. A few more kids did the same, then Naramutro swooped, caught, and tossed. It seemed too simple: everyone was taking turns; there was no longer any apparent competition.

While he waited his next turn, he saw Ama circling

above. Her face was creased with worry—she shouted something to him, but he couldn't hear. He looked for Elli but didn't see her.

Slowly he became aware that, one by one, the others were dropping out of the game, pulling up to fly in lazy circles above the dwindling number of players below, so his turn, and Naramutro's, came closer and closer together. Finally, only they were left. All the other flyers watched from above, scattered across the sky below the increasingly distant diffusers.

Taj's arms and chest were beginning to hurt, but he wouldn't give up. When the other boy swooped under him to catch the ball he saw that Naramutro's face was set in fierce concentration, mixed with what looked like increasing desperation.

They spiraled lower and lower. Taj's breath came raggedly and his chest muscles felt like they were on fire. It was getting harder and harder to move his flight wings.

Then, abruptly, it was over. Naramutro tossed the ball down and then groaned in defeat as Taj swooped down and caught it. The other boy turned and climbed slowly away.

Taj turned to follow, but his wings felt strangely heavy. Naramutro seemed to be climbing faster now, and Taj couldn't keep up—he wasn't even sure he was really climbing.

A few minutes later he was sure he wasn't—no matter what he did, he kept sinking. He could barely move his flight wings now; they felt like lead.

Suddenly the ball still held in his scoop expanded with a loud pop and escaped. Startled, Taj watched it dwindle swiftly upward, toward the aerie now lost in the dazzle of the diffusers high above.

And then he remembered. "*. . . The farther an object is from the spin axis—the lower it is—the heavier it gets, and the change with altitude is much greater than on a planet or in a gravitor-equipped habitat.*" Now he knew why Gee-Em had been so insistent about the orientation vid.

With a muffled crack, his lift wings collapsed and the rushing air forced his flight wings and arms up over his head. He was falling. The surface of Talajara rushed up to meet him.

Suraki.

Icarus inverted.

He'd flown too low.

Then something slapped at him in a vicious double concussion and he passed out.

Taj opened his eyes and blinked in confusion. He was floating in the center of the strangest room he'd ever seen, with furniture, plants, tapestries, paintings and statues, and even bookcases on every surface. He couldn't figure out where the floor was, or the ceiling, or if those terms even meant anything here.

Hearing a rustle of cloth, he turned. Beside him was Gee-Em, but her bubble was nowhere to be seen, and Taj realized he was in her home at the spin axis of Talajara. The double concussion that knocked him out must have been her geebubble accelerating to transonic speed to rescue him.

She looked at him in silence for a long time.

"You didn't watch the orientation, did you? You didn't know about the Suraki Effect."

Taj felt his face flush. "Not the whole thing. When they mentioned Icarus, I . . . uhh . . . They called me Icky at school. I didn't want to hear about it." Taj felt his eyes burning; he resolved fiercely that he wasn't going to cry. Gee-Em would never sponsor him to a commission now, not after such a stupid mistake.

"I've seen your simulator tapes, both naval and flight," she said. "You are quite good, actually. There was really only one lesson remaining, although I had not intended it to be quite so dramatic."

Taj felt his throat closing up with the effort not to weep. "Wha . . . what?" he choked out.

Her fierce blue eyes transfixed him. "You tell me." Her voice was flat.

Oh, Telos, he hated it when adults did this. He opened his mouth to reply that he'd learned that gravity in a highdwelling changed far faster with altitude than on a planet, but he stopped himself. Meeting her merciless gaze, he knew that wasn't the answer. He'd known that, but he'd still almost killed himself.

But what *did* she want? If he didn't answer correctly, he knew she'd write him off without hesitation.

Unbidden, Mari's voice came back to him. *"But you're a downsider, and so is Flugel."*

Flugel had thought the WingWorld sim would teach him what he needed to know, but WingWorld was a hollowed-out asteroid with a gravity generator at its center—fourspace-distortion gravity, like a planet, with the same almost imperceptible gradient with altitude. There was no Suraki Effect.

But Flugel was a downsider and hadn't thought of the Suraki Effect. Or hadn't known.

Suddenly it was clear.

"No matter how real it seems, a sim is just someone else's idea of reality," said Taj. "If they don't know something, or overlook it, it won't be there, and you can't learn it." He thought a moment longer, encouraged by the first hint of a smile on the nuller's deeply lined face.

"And what they don't know can kill you."

Gee-Em smiled broadly. "You'll do, Tajarivani. I've known a few naval officers who learned that lesson only too late, so you'll be ahead of the game at the Academy." She reached over and tabbed a control on a legless table floating nearby.

"Now greet your friends, who've been *really* worried about you."

Ama, Elli, and Tulli came in, followed, to Taj's amazement, by Naramutro. Taj laughed. Somehow, he was sure he wouldn't be seeing the inside of a simulator again until he got to the Academy.

And that was just fine with him.

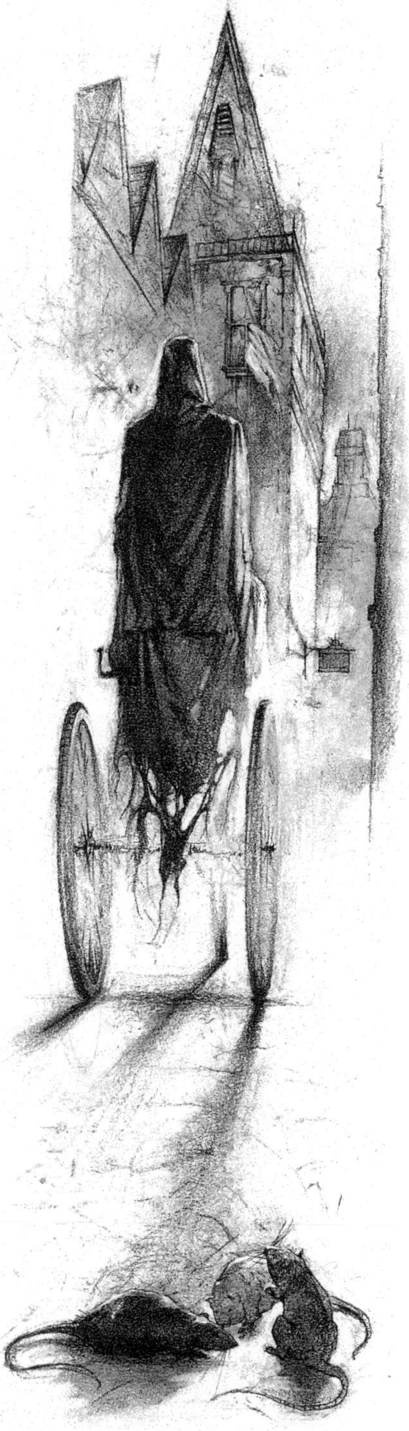

DAN BENNETT

ON PERDITION

"Red!" Smoki called over the din of the crowd. "The gents'! Grab your tools and do your job, kid!"

My "tools" were a mop and a bucket.

You can guess what my job was.

I tried to disappear into a corner, but thanks to my hair Smoki had no trouble spotting me.

Nobody *ever* has trouble spotting me. Almost everyone

on Perdition has black hair and brown eyes, so my bright orange locks and green eyes mean I get a hard time from just about everybody. They say my dad must've been a spacer who was just passing through. I used to believe they were right.

Given the chance, I wouldn't have picked swamping out the johns in Smoki's Bar as my number-one career choice. But who has a choice? I sleep in a storeroom at the back of a pub, I go to bed smelling like you-don't-want-to-know, but at least I've *got* a place to sleep. And on top of that, Smoki gives me enough vouchers to buy three meals a day from the protein synth down the street.

Which means I don't get weak from hunger and pass out on a regular basis. Which means I've got it a whole lot better than some other fifteen-year-olds on Perdition. A far-fringe colony planet isn't a place for youngsters, but the grown-ups sure keep Perdition stocked with fresh ones. It seems like they can't keep away from each other—but they sure find it easy to stay away from the babies they make together.

Me, I don't even know who my parents are. My earliest memories are all of the government-run homes for the "unparented" (that's what they call us, as if babies come from nowhere). I spent all my time in those places until I hit the big One-Three—once you become a teenager, you're given a scant handful of vouchers, and you're out on the street to make room for the new kiddies that keep coming.

So, no, I don't know who Ma and Pa are. But I don't daydream about them, the way some kids do. I know my folks aren't secretly spies or high government officials who hid me on Perdition to keep me safe. I know they aren't going to show up tomorrow to take me away from here and buy me real food and clothes that fit—and if they tried, I'd probably spit in their eyes. After all these years, I wouldn't know how to act if somebody tried to do something nice for me.

I'd still be on the street—or dead, maybe—if Smoki hadn't found me sleeping in an empty recycling bin behind her bar. She scratched her razor-stubbled head with one long fingernail and said, "Kid, if you're gonna flop on my property, you're gonna have to pay rent or go to work." That night, I swept, mopped, and otherwise scrubbed that place until my hands were blistered. Worked harder than I ever had in my life. I also slept under a roof for the first time in nearly a year.

Problem was, Smoki got to thinking she'd made an investment in me—like she'd bought the right to comment on how I lived my life, and I guess in a way she had. So she wasn't shy about speaking her mind when I started nagging her about making my bones.

That's how you get a better job than mopping a bar—you make your bones. Which usually means killing somebody.

See, life on Perdition is all about fear—there isn't any money, really, except at the highest levels. The way to be rich around here is to have lots of people scared of you. You get what you want because other folks are afraid of what will happen to them if you don't. Get rich enough that way, and pretty soon you need other people to do your scaring for you. That's where the real opportunities are for people like me.

"You're gonna be on my back about this until I cave in, aren't you, Red?" she said one night after closing time. I brought her the last tray of empty glasses, and she began sorting the ones that needed to be washed from the ones she thought could pass as clean another night. "Just gotta do it, don't you? Gotta make your bones and be a big gun. You just make sure it's what you want, kid. There's other ways to make it outta the pits. If anybody could do it, you could."

But it's been a long time since Smoki was on the streets. She has no idea how hard it is to get something better for yourself these days.

And I don't really have a problem with the idea of shutting somebody down—it doesn't mean that much to do murders in a place where anybody can die anytime. And on Perdition, sometimes dying is better.

So I was ready when Smoki finally called me behind the bar this morning. She said she knew a guy who had a job for me. Seems that Syl Braga, the guy Smoki pays to make sure her bar is still standing when she comes to work each morning, had a fallout with a biz partner. Braga wanted this partner of his to go away on a long-term basis. Like forever.

Braga showed up late this afternoon with a big mute bodyguard. Smoki showed them to a booth with a good view of the front door, then she called me over. She made the introductions, then walked off without another word.

Braga told me the unlucky target of his distaste was Luce Cavek, the proprietor of a dingy restaurant called the Fallen Angel. Cavek would catch a pedicab this evening after having dinner at the Angel, like she did every night. The plan was for me to replace the kid who usually pedaled Cavek to her apartment a few blocks away. I'd take the not-too-scenic route through the city's Dead Zone and shut Cavek down where nobody would ask questions.

"Consider yourself lucky, Red," Braga told me. "Luce Cavek is tough. She got where she is on the same road you're taking. But sometimes money and power make people think they're bulletproof. She's gotten so sure of herself she doesn't even keep a guard with her. By the time she figures out what's coming around, your job'll be done and you'll be hoofing it back here. Anybody asks, Smoki will tell 'em you been right here all night."

Then Braga handed me a duster. Dusters are little one-shot guns that blast a cloud of nasty poison crystals, like shattering glass. The crystals dissolve in blood, and whoever catches the blast is gone before the dust settles. Old-fashioned, but plenty effective.

"This baby's a positive outlaw, Red," Braga said when he slipped the thing to me, making sure the table between us hid his hands, "so ditch it when you're through. Get caught with it, and I don't know you. I don't know you, I can't help you, and neither can your boss. See?"

"Saw," I said. I checked the duster's safety cap, then I stuffed it in a pocket and headed for the pedicab station.

"It's not too late to back out of this, Red," Smoki said when I was halfway out the door. She didn't look up from the glass she was washing. "This kind of thing changes people sometimes. I just hope I'll still know you when it's done."

I just smiled like I knew what I was doing.

It took me a couple of minutes to find Luce Cavek's usual driver. The cab stand is always surrounded by streetlings looking for work; it's no big surprise to see three times as many kids milling about under the sick fluorescent lights of the stand as there are cabs to pedal. I picked through three or four tight clumps of skinny, snot-nosed waifs before I found the kid I was looking for.

"Syl Braga sent me," I said for what felt like the hundredth time, expecting another blank stare or another kick in the shin. Instead, the kid grinned around a set of yellow teeth.

"Where's my payoff?" she demanded, and I handed her the bundle of vouchers Braga had given me.

"Okay, listen up," the kid said. "Luce Cavek always wears a hooded cape and dark shades, like a 3Vid star, and she walks like she owns the world. Barks when she talks. You can't miss her."

She jammed her cabbie's cap on my head and pulled the flaps down.

"It's warm out, but keep those flaps where they are," she said. "Wouldn't be too cool for anybody to spot that hair of yours while you're doing your job tonight, would it?"

I climbed into the seat of her pedicab, and she shook her head. "You gotta be crazy to take on Luce Cavek."

"Mind your own," I said, and I was surprised at how tough and steady my voice was, seeing as how I was scared boneless. I started pedaling and swung the cab toward the Fallen Angel.

The narrow driver's seat was starting to make my own seat sore when Cavek finally breezed out the door of her restaurant. She looked down through her shades at the street people as if she was three meters tall and gliding above it all. Like she was hearing music somebody had written just for her. Obviously, she thought she was a major attraction.

"You're not the usual kid," she said when she got in the back of the cab.

"She's sick," I told her. "I'm filling in."

"She knows when to shut up and when to pedal," she said, and her voice was like ice on the back of my neck. "Let's see if you do. Now get rolling before I decide to have you killed out of sheer boredom."

I pumped the pedals and pulled away from the curb, thinking it was going to be easy to pop the duster on this woman.

I had just gotten us up to street speed when her comm card chimed. She let it go for half a minute, letting the person on the other end stew a bit, before she answered.

"Cavek," she said in that same cold voice. She listened a minute, then she said, "So kill him. What's the problem?"

Another pause, then she was saying, "I *know* who he is. He saved my life two years ago. I don't need you to tell me that. But what has he done for me this quarter?"

I turned the cab toward the Dead Zone. We zipped past the signs that say "WARNING: NOW ENTERING A NON-PATROLLED ZONE. PROCEED AT OWN RISK."

Cavek was too busy to notice when the street started getting rougher. We bumped through little hills of garbage, dipped into blackened holes left in the concrete during the last food riots, and she kept barking into the comm card.

"It's okay," she said, "I understand. If you can't do it, you can't do it. I'll just have to find someone else who can shut you *and* him down."

A very brief silence, then she said, "I knew you'd see it my way." And she slipped the comm card back into her pocket.

That's when she noticed where we were.

"You're going the wrong way." She slapped the back of my head with a gloved hand. "If you think I live in the Zone, you're even more ignorant than you look."

"Sorry," I said, trying to sound stupid instead of scared. "I thought I was supposed to take the shortest route—"

"The shortest route that won't get me killed, you idiot! Don't you know where we are?"

I took a few more turns. It wasn't too hard to pretend I was lost. I'd never been so deep into the Zone. The place was like an ancient, crumbling battlefield—but with fewer street signs.

I pulled up short in a blind alley, and Cavek slapped me again.

"Are you deaf *and* blind?" She was finally losing some of her cool.

I turned the cab's handlebars hard, swinging back toward the mouth of the alley, which was just visible as a patch of gray in all the blackness. I couldn't see a working streetlight in any direction. People began stepping out of the shadows, eyeing the cab and thinking maybe they were going to eat tonight.

When Cavek hit me a third time, I squeezed the hand brakes and brought the cab to a skidding stop.

I turned on the narrow seat, sticking a shaking hand into my pocket for the duster. It was time to do the job.

Cavek was livid. She whipped the hood back and yanked her shades off.

Bright red hair fell down around her shoulders, and she glared at me with green eyes.

When I got back home, I stepped behind the bar and slipped the duster to Smoki. Her eyes went wide for a second, and she was ready to pitch a fit until she noticed the duster hadn't been fired. She smiled when she saw that. But she didn't say a word. So now I have another reason to be grateful to Smoki.

I realize Syl Braga will probably just find somebody else to do the job I couldn't do. But it won't be me, and that's all that matters.

I know what you're thinking, but it's not because Luce Cavek could be my mother. She probably is, but that doesn't mean I owe her anything. She never did anything for me but give birth fifteen years ago, and she wasn't exactly doing me a favor then.

So it wasn't blood that kept me from popping the duster. It's just that it was too easy to see myself in her shoes a decade or so down the road.

I don't ever want to have anything more in common with that woman. The red hair, the green eyes are enough.

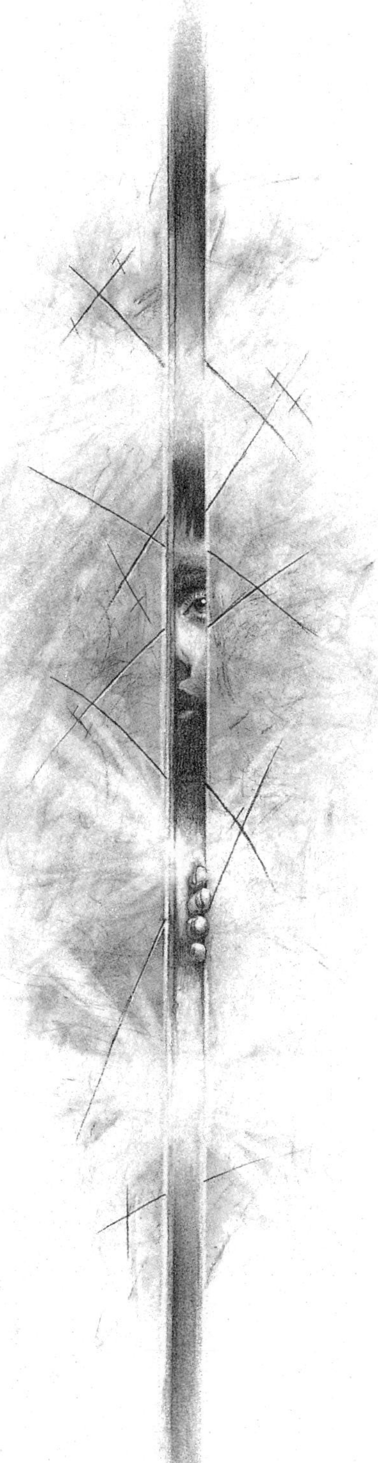

Debra Doyle and
James D. Macdonald

Crossover

Down the corridor there's a door, and the door doesn't open.

The lights behind the panels overhead are pale blue. That's different from all the other corridors in the station, where the doors open for anyone—they're just to control loss of pressure, *those* doors, and the lights in the panels above them are white or yellow.

The white and yellow lights

in the station are supposed to be like the star Merilee has never seen. The teachers say that the lights keep people from getting sick. And they do—she's seen accidents and injuries sometimes, but no one she knows has ever been sick.

Sometimes Merilee goes down the corridor with the blue lights and presses her hand against the door. The door feels cool to her touch and the steel hums under her fingertips like it does everywhere else in the station. She waits at the door for a minute—or two—or many—and then walks on. Sometimes she goes to the store, sometimes she goes to the school, sometimes she goes to the video gallery or the park or the rec center, and sometimes she even goes home.

She has to be at home or at some authorized activity before the night comes. At night the lights get turned off and the doors stop opening and closing. Those are the rules and everyone obeys them. She wonders what it would be like to be out at night, when the doors don't work—and she imagines being stuck in the Long Corridor, ninety meters door to door, with nothing to look at and nowhere to sit for twelve straight hours.

There's only one locked door that she's ever seen, though. That's the one at the end of the blue corridor. Everyone knows that the doors don't work at night, so no one ever leaves their home or their authorized activity after the lights go out. There's a lot of paperwork involved in getting to an activity, too, so most of the time people stay at home and don't bother. Merilee wonders about the term *paperwork*—she's never seen a piece of paper in her life, even though the teachers talk about it all the time—but she doesn't wonder about it much. She doesn't wonder about words like *steel,* or *gravity,* or *ci-space* either. Instead she wonders about the closed door.

And in her wondering, she wonders if opposites happen. If when the lights go dim in the rest of the station, they blaze up in the blue corridor. Or if, when all the rest of the doors stay sealed, this door—the sealed one—unlocks. And They come through.

Merilee is imaginative. The teachers all say so. They praise her for telling clever stories, even though they never believe in them. "It's just Merilee," they say. "Making things up again."

Now she imagines what might be living on the other side of the locked door. More little girls like herself, maybe, with parents and brothers, little girls who go to school and home and authorized activities. And she imagines that when the lights get bright in the dim blue corridor, this door opens up for the people on the other side, and they come through the door into the station and walk up to the *next* door, the one that opens and shuts for anybody on this side in the daytime, and find it locked.

Maybe, she thinks, this one piece of corridor, only twenty meters long, is the overlap where she walks during the daytime and They walk at night.

No one but Merilee is interested in the corridor. At least, she's never seen anyone else down there. Maybe there's only one little girl on the other side who's interested in coming down this corridor, just one, who walks the twenty meters under the blue lights and puts her hand against the closed door to the main passage and wonders what's on the other side.

Merilee would like to make friends with that girl.

But Merilee is quite grown-up and intelligent, and she knows that this is all imagination. She turns away from the locked door and walks back toward the main passage. The door opens at her approach, and she goes farther, turning right and walking to the store, and then going back home.

Then comes the day of the scratch.

She finds a scratch on the wall—on the unscratchable metal—a scratch that begins on one side of the door and continues into it, past the airtight seal.

So the door has been opened, and something has come through. There *is* something. But how far had They come? Merilee walks back again toward the main passage. The door there unseals itself at her approach. She is an authorized person.

Did the others come this far? Did they see this door to the main passage as the one that would not open, the door with the mysterious country on the far side?

She decides to leave a scratch herself—a mark on the wall to tell them that someone has come by, that there is a way into the next land, into the passage beyond and then to her quarters.

Nothing in her backpack or her pockets will scratch the bulkhead. The metal resists every tool she has at hand. There is a chance she can borrow a tool, but a bigger chance that she will be caught doing it, caught and asked why a girl her age needs a diamond-bitted cutting rig, and Merilee is a poor liar. Nobody ever believes her stories, even when they're mostly true.

So instead, low down on the wall where no one but a child like herself would see it, she draws a line in colored wax with her marker: a little horizontal line, running into the gap where the door fits into the wall when it seals shut. A line pointing the way through the door and out into the main passage.

Then she goes away and waits, waits for the night to come and go, so her steps can take her again to the blue passageway. Her mark is still there. And a new scratch goes across it at a right angle, making a plus sign out of scratched metal and colored wax. The mark is a tiny thing—she never would have seen it if she hadn't been looking closely—but it's fresh. With her marker, Merilee draws a linc of colored wax across either end of the new scratch.

Then she walks down the twenty meters of corridor, under the blue lights, and finds the scratch on the sealed door. She draws a line through it, making another plus sign out of scratched metal and colored wax. Then she goes home.

The next morning, she finds a crossbar at the end of each of her marks, scratched in the unbreakable surface of the wall. She caps each of the crossing lines with a right-angle line of her own. And the next morning, each of her capping lines is itself capped with a slash of scratched metal. She crosses them, and the next morning the crosses are recrossed. Little patches of lines and crossmarks grow on the walls.

No one notices. No one comes here except Merilee—and now she is determined to meet her friend, face-to-face.

That the passageway lies open to the other side during the nighttime is obvious. But how to be there during the night? Since no doors open and close in the nighttime, she will have to come there during the day and conceal herself somewhere in those twenty meters of passageway—hidden in a place with no hiding places—until the lights go off in the station and the doors stop working. And she will have to fool her parents, both on the night before and on the morning after, so that they won't notice her absence and become worried.

This problem frustrates her for quite a while. She daydreams in school about ways to get to the twenty meters of passageway. She nightdreams about it too. She waits and watches, and draws lines, and visits the sealed doorway whenever she has a chance.

And on one of those visits, the loss-of-pressure alarm sounds in the station. Loss of pressure is a serious thing, and nobody on the station ever says whether the alarms are drills or not. This time is no different from the other times—all the doors in all the corridors sigh closed and lock down tight, with a click of metal sliding into metal.

Merilee knows that she's stuck in the tunnel until the alert is over and the doors unlock. She sits against the wall and reads her schoolbooks by the blue light overhead until she can't stand it anymore. Then she notices that she's hungry and thirsty, but there's no help for it, because she's alone in the twenty meters of corridor and all the doors are locked.

More time passes, and she sleeps, curled up against the wall, until dimly through the door she hears the all-clear sound. When the door into the main passageway doesn't open for her, even though the all-clear has sounded, she knows that this is the nighttime—and she is where she wanted to be, outside the sealed door.

The lights come up. The blue passageway, always blue and nightdim before, becomes as bright as day, bright enough to hurt her eyes after all the time in the dimness.

Leaving her pack and the books where she has been sitting, she stands and stretches and walks toward the door that has never opened for her before. The door opens, and she sees that strange place beyond. The place is new, newer than the part of the base she is used to, but otherwise the same, with its walls and lights and sliding doors.

She hears a sound, as of someone walking, breathing, in the new base section, and turns toward the noise. A girl who looks just like Merilee is coming, dressed the same way, with the same hair and eyes that she recognizes from pictures of herself.

"Hello," Merilee says. "How is it that you look just like me?"

"Better to ask how I speak your language," the stranger says.

"How *do* you speak my language?"

The stranger doesn't answer directly. "Better to ask how you can breathe the same kind of air I do."

"How can you and I breathe the same kind of air?"

"Better you should ask what I really look like," the stranger says.

"Fine," Merilee says. She is growing impatient. "What do you look like?"

And the stranger shows her.

When it's over, she's out in the twenty-meter passage again, waiting until the last moment before the nighttime. She darts outside and hides in the main passage when the nightdim comes.

Once all the good people have gone home, or to their authorized activities, she goes back to her own house, and finds that in the nightdim time her parents are the same as in the daybright time, except that they had lost her and missed her, and now she is back.

"Where were you?" they ask.

"I was locked up in the blue passageway," she says. And then she tells a lie—the first good lie she's ever told, the first lie of hers that anybody has ever believed. "But nothing happened."

Janni Lee Simner

Exchange Student

Tomas Alvarov was the cutest guy in the ninth grade. Blond hair, broad shoulders, blue eyes to die for. Trouble was, he wouldn't be born for fifty years.

No one knew that last part, of course, and I wasn't allowed to tell them. Just like I couldn't tell them why he showed up dressed all wrong the first day of class. He wore tight shorts that barely covered his butt and some white puffy things around his wrists—nothing else. A few kids laughed when he entered the room; someone whistled. He stared at them through fierce eyes, not understanding what was so funny but daring them to make something of it, anyway.

Our homeroom teacher, Mrs. Ambrose, turned red when she saw him, a slow blush that crept up her cheeks to the roots of her gray hair. She grabbed Tomas's arm and dragged him from the room.

When Tomas returned, he wore a loose black T-shirt and tattered sneakers; together they made the shorts look almost decent.

Mrs. Ambrose explained that Tomas came from Arakistan, a small ex-Soviet republic that didn't make the news much. He'd been sent as part of an exchange program, and she hoped we would all treat him well.

What she didn't explain was why someone from Russia would run around half-naked in autumn. I thought someone would ask, but no one did. Then again, I also thought someone would figure out that there was no such place as Arakistan and never had been, and that never happened, either.

Tomas Alvarov came from Brooklyn. I guessed from his clothes—or lack of them—that it had been summer when he'd left. Not summer 1995, though. Summer 2060.

I waited for Tomas outside the school gates. The air held the crisp, burnt smell of winter, even though it was only September. The distant mountains were a blaze of red and yellow leaves.

Just before lunch I'd managed to introduce myself

to Tomas, explaining that Mom and I were his host family and he should meet me after school. What I didn't get to ask was why he'd shown up two days late; we'd been waiting since Saturday, after all. Too many other kids kept crowding around him and getting in the way. Nothing like good looks to help a guy make friends fast.

"Hi, Suzie." Krista Arrens walked up beside me and dropped her books to the ground. "Your guest's popular. Unlike some of us." Her freckled face held a wistful expression I knew much too well. Krista always complained about not being popular. It bugged me sometimes. I was her friend, after all. Didn't that count for something?

I turned away from Krista and back toward the school, pushing my braid over one shoulder. Tomas was standing in front of the building now. He must have just come out. I waved him over.

He walked slowly, with uneven steps and an awkward tension in his shoulders. Maybe he wasn't used to wearing clothes this time of year. Maybe the sneakers Mrs. Ambrose had found him were too tight. I wondered why the Institute hadn't shown him how to dress. Then again, his mistake hadn't kept him from getting along with the other kids.

"Hello," Tomas said. "Sorry to make you wait." He had a funny accent, different from my relatives' in New York City. But his English was fine, at any rate. He smiled. He'd been smiling a lot that day. He liked having people pay attention to him.

"No problem." I smiled back—it seemed rude not to—and started toward home. Tomas and Krista followed.

"Where's your car?" Tomas asked. Leaves crunched beneath his feet.

"My what?"

Tomas fixed me with his intent blue gaze. "You're old enough to drive, aren't you? Fourteen?"

"Fifteen. Driving age is sixteen here." And even if I were old enough, Mom wouldn't get me a car just because I could drive one.

"Oh." Tomas looked disappointed. "Can't you at least drive an electric scooter?"

"Is that what you drive in Arakistan?" Krista's face showed real interest. I'd almost forgotten she didn't know where Tomas really came from.

Tomas hesitated. Then he nodded, blond hair brushing his neck. "Yes. Yes, it is."

"What's Arakistan like?" There was a dreamy edge to Krista's voice. I wished I could tell her the truth.

"It's different," Tomas said. Krista kept staring at him, so he added, "Different from here." A blush crept up his face. He walked faster. Krista matched his pace, leaving me behind.

For a moment I just watched them. There was still something strange about the way Tomas walked; he already seemed tired, even though we hadn't gone very far. Maybe walking wasn't something he did much. Maybe that was why he'd expected me to have a car. Beside him, Krista walked lightly, keeping up a steady stream of conversation. I hurried to catch up. I had plenty of questions of my own, but those would have to wait until later.

I thought about how the Cornell Time Institute first contacted Mom late last spring. The Institute had talked to the principal first, of course. I don't know how they convinced Mr. Phillips they were serious, but they did. Mr. Phillips had called Mom, asking if she'd host an Institute student. Mom was on the school board then—her law firm hadn't promoted her to partner yet, so she still had the time—which was why he'd thought of her.

"It all sounds pretty unlikely," Mom had said to me at the time, "but Mr. Phillips isn't creative enough to make something like that up. I told him I'd at least listen to what the Institute has to say."

Somehow, the Institute had convinced Mom, too. I don't know what they told her, and she wouldn't say. But the next thing I knew, we were making plans to have someone stay with us in the fall.

I'd had a lot more trouble believing it than Mom. I still had trouble, even though I'd had time to get used to the idea. I looked at Tomas, walking along beside me. He kept glancing around—was he taking in the details of our time, comparing them to his own? Had he really come back more than fifty years?

I wanted to ask, but I couldn't, not now. The Institute had made Mom and Mr. Phillips agree not to tell anyone else about the program. Mom had told me anyway, but she'd made me promise not to tell anyone else. Not even Krista.

Mom was waiting when we got home. I'd called her from school, letting her know that Tomas had finally shown up. She'd been as curious as I was about why he was late. Anyway, she'd taken off work early to meet him. She still wore her work skirt and blouse, but she'd wiped off her makeup and switched from her pumps into tennis shoes. From the kitchen I smelled the spicy tang of dinner cooking. Chicken, with stuffing of some sort. Mom hardly ever cooked from scratch.

"Hello, Tomas," Mom said, holding out a hand. Tomas hesitated, then took it. I wondered if people still shook hands in Tomas's time. Even if they didn't, the Institute would have taught him what to do, wouldn't they?

Sure they would. Just like they'd taught him how to dress. They might be good at time travel, but they didn't seem very good at the other stuff that went with it.

"Well, I know you must be tired," Mom said. "Why don't I just show you your room, and then you can have dinner and unwind?" Tomas nodded, and Mom led him up the stairs. I realized he didn't have any luggage. Was he supposed to buy all his clothes here?

I grabbed an armful of dishes from the cupboard and began setting the dining-room table. Krista wandered over to the phone to ask her parents if she could stay for supper. For once, I wished she weren't staying—I wanted to talk to Tomas—but I couldn't think of a good reason to make her leave.

As soon as we sat down to dinner, Krista began asking about Arakistan again. Tomas replied between bites, mostly yes and no answers. He finished a chicken leg, reached for another. "This is really good," he said. "What brand is it?"

I laughed. Usually dinner did come out of a box—Swanson or Banquet or whatever. "Mom brand," I said. I guess Tomas's parents didn't cook much, either.

"Never heard of it." Tomas's voice was perfectly

serious, his gaze so earnest that I giggled. I couldn't help it.

Mom cast a warning glance in my direction. "Kimberly Susan Wilkins—" I knew that tone well enough. I swallowed the rest of my laughter. Mom turned to Tomas and explained, "I can't cook every night, but it is your first day, after all. And since I got off work early—"

Tomas had stopped eating. A half-chewed drumstick dangled from his fingers; his mouth hung open. He stared at me. He didn't seem to hear Mom at all.

"You're Kimberly Wilkins?"

"Suzie. No one calls me Kimberly." Not if they want to stay on speaking terms, anyway.

"But they will," Tomas said. His eyes were suddenly bright; there was something like awe in his voice. "That's the name you'll use when—"

A sudden crash made me jump. Mom had spilled her glass. She stood, Diet Coke dripping from her blouse. "Get me a towel," she said. Her voice sounded tight and angry. Mom never spilled anything.

I nodded, backing toward the kitchen. What had Tomas been about to say?

I found a towel in the cupboard, but Mom came up behind me and pulled it from my hands. "We need to talk." She spoke in the low voice that meant she wasn't angry after all, just serious and a little worried. I closed the cupboard door and leaned back against the counter.

Mom looked down at me. "He's not supposed to talk about things like that, you know. That's one of the first things the Institute explained."

"Things like what?" I asked, though I suspected I already knew.

"The Institute trains its students not to reveal the future. Not politics, not who's going to be famous, not what people are going to do with their lives. Not anything."

I stared at the floor, an uneasy tingling beginning at the base of my skull. I wished Mom hadn't cut Tomas off.

I thought back to the time, a couple of years ago now, when the vice-president had come to speak at my school. When he was done talking, I'd gotten to shake his hand. The look on Tomas's face had matched the way I'd felt that day—shy and startled, not quite able to believe someone so important could exist for real and not just on TV.

Who the hell did Tomas think I was? Who did he think I would be, fifty years from now? I shivered. For a moment I wondered whether I wanted to know—I could be someone awful, after all—but I pushed the thought aside. Of course I wanted to know. I wanted it more badly every moment I thought about it.

"What do you think he was going to say?" I asked.

"It's not important." Mom set her mouth in a thin, determined line. "If it affects us, we'll find out soon enough. If it doesn't, then it's none of our business, anyway."

But it was my business, mine more than anyone else's. I opened my mouth to argue, but Mom kept talking in that low, steady voice.

"I'll talk with Tomas later. In the meantime I want you to promise me something."

A cold lump settled in my stomach. I knew what she was going to say.

"Promise you won't ask Tomas to tell you anything else. Even if he offers to."

I bit my lip.

"Suzie?"

I swallowed. Once I made a promise, Mom expected me to keep it, no matter what. "All right," I said, but I avoided Mom's gaze. For the first time in my life, I wasn't sure I'd be able to keep my word.

Mom went upstairs to change out of her damp blouse; I went back to the dining room. Krista and Tomas weren't at the table.

Krista stood by the phone, talking angrily into the receiver. "I want you to pick me up now," she yelled. "Not in fifteen minutes." Tomas stood beside her, looking confused.

"What's wrong?" I asked. I hadn't been gone all that long, after all.

"She asked me about her future." Tomas shrugged, daring me to make something of it.

I felt a sudden burst of anger. Tomas had told Krista what he hadn't told me—and Krista wasn't even supposed to know where Tomas came from.

Krista slammed the phone down. Her face had turned so fierce a red that I couldn't see her freckles. "He told me you were going to be important one day. Of course I didn't take him seriously, but just for the heck of it, I asked about me."

Krista didn't know, then. To her it was just some sort of joke, a game. The fact didn't make me feel any better.

"What'd he say?"

Krista took a deep breath. "He said he'd never heard of me! He said I probably wouldn't do anything that mattered." She glared at Tomas.

I wondered why she cared what he said. She didn't know that he'd come from the future, that he might know what he was talking about. I did, and I wasn't even allowed to ask any questions. It wasn't fair.

"I'm going outside to wait for Dad," Krista said. I knew that I should follow her, talk to her until she felt less upset, but I didn't. I wanted to stay with Tomas. Maybe, if I pushed the conversation in the right direction, he'd drop some hints. I stood there, waiting for Krista to leave.

She finally did, glancing back with a watery, hurt look. I didn't know whether the look was aimed at Tomas or at me. She walked out slowly, slamming the door behind her.

Mom walked in as soon as Krista left. So much for talking to Tomas.

"Krista gone already?" she asked. I nodded. Mom had changed out of her work clothes into a gray sweatsuit.

"We need to talk," she told Tomas. Tomas shrugged and followed her to the table. The dishes were still piled there, but Mom didn't seem to care.

I moved to sit with them, but Mom waved me away. "Don't you have some homework to do?" Her low tone meant I'd better find some, even if I didn't. She wanted to talk to Tomas alone. I climbed the stairs slowly, straining to hear them. All I made out were muffled whispers. I waited at the top step for a long time, but they didn't get any louder.

Finally I went into my room and flopped down on the bed. Mom had brought my schoolbooks up; they lay in a neat pile on my pillow. I stared at the thick spines: math, science, English, history, French. Did the key to my future lie in one of those books? I liked history well enough. Maybe I'd be a politician, maybe president. I didn't like talking to strangers, though, and the president was always talking to someone or other. Science? Chemistry was fun, but chemists probably had to be good at math. I couldn't think of any famous chemists, anyway.

I shoved the books off the bed; they fell to the carpet with a thud. I stared where they lay scattered.

Math was the only class I'd ever failed, but there was nothing I was so good at that I could see spending the rest of my life at it. One day I'd graduate high school, though, and then I'd have to decide what to do next—a thought that scared me more than I liked to admit.

Tomas already knew what I'd do next. If he'd tell me, I wouldn't have to worry about it. I'd know what decisions to make.

The tingling at the back of my neck started up again. I didn't just want to know. I had to know—so badly I could taste it, a sharp, bitter tang at the back of my throat. I needed answers, and I couldn't wait fifty years. I had too much to figure out before then.

I thought of Krista, storming out the front door. Mom hadn't said anything about Krista asking questions. If she asked for me, I wouldn't be breaking my word.

That was assuming Krista would agree, though. Assuming she was no longer angry at Tomas—and no longer angry at me.

Krista ignored me all morning, then sat down beside me at lunch as if nothing had happened. I should have guessed she would. Krista hated sitting alone.

Tomas sat a couple of tables away. A bunch of kids sat with him, talking in loud voices. He seemed perfectly comfortable, as if he'd known them all for years. Only his eyes gave him away. They flickered from person to person, taking things in with a strange, eager intensity. As if he were determined to learn all he could about them—or not to make any mistakes. I couldn't tell which.

I smushed my mashed potatoes beneath my fork, wondering whether I dared ask Krista to talk to him. I didn't want to get her upset all over again. I felt bad enough for not following her outside last night.

Then again, Tomas was sitting there, so close. If only she would ask—just one question, that's all it would take. I swallowed. "Krista—" I began.

"Don't call me a loser, loser!" The yell came from Tomas's table. I heard a crash and realized that someone had stood, knocking his chair over behind him. Suddenly everyone was yelling at once. Somehow I knew that Tomas had started the commotion, though I couldn't imagine how. A moment ago everything had been fine. I dropped my fork and ran over.

Most of the kids were standing by the time I got there; Tomas was rubbing his chin. Someone had punched him. "Chill out," a girl said, but nobody paid any attention.

I heard Krista giggling behind me.

"What's so funny?"

"It worked," Krista whispered. "Now the popular kids don't like him any more than they like us."

I turned to face her. "What did you do?" My voice came out hard and cold, like steel. Getting mad at someone was one thing. Getting them into a fight so bad they got hurt was another.

"Just dropped a few hints. Told people what sort of questions to ask. I figured if other people got half as angry as I did last night, he'd be in big trouble."

I wanted to wipe the smug grin off Krista's face. Instead I turned back to the crowd.

"He's only kidding," I said. "He pulled the same thing over at my place last night." The excuse sounded stupid, but I couldn't think of anything else that might help Tomas out.

"Being told we're all going to fail isn't funny." A strange, bitter tone crept into the speaker's voice. "I can fail just fine on my own."

"I didn't say that," Tomas insisted weakly. I barely heard him. A cold feeling settled in the pit of my stomach. I suddenly understood why everyone—including Krista—had gotten so angry.

Last night I'd stayed awake past midnight, past when Tomas went to bed and Mom turned out the lights. I'd stared into the dark, trying to imagine ever being good at anything—really good, good enough to be famous. I couldn't. Even though Tomas had just about said that would happen.

How would I have felt if instead Tomas had said I'd fail? Even if I hadn't believed him, hadn't realized he might know what he was talking about, I would have been angry. I was scared enough of failing already.

I stepped forward and grabbed Tomas's arm. "We need to talk," I said, startled at how much my voice sounded like Mom's.

To my surprise, no one stopped me as I dragged Tomas from the cafeteria.

We found an empty classroom. I sat on the edge of the teacher's desk; Tomas took one of the chairs. My legs swung above the floor, and I had to look down to talk to him. I felt funny, like a parent lecturing a kid.

"I thought Mom talked to you last night. I thought she told you not to say anything about the future."

"I didn't give anything away." Tomas looked puzzled again. "It's not my fault people got mad."

"Whether or not you gave something away isn't the point." I wondered whether I meant that. He'd almost given something away last night. I still wanted to know, but I'd worry about that later.

Tomas rubbed his face. A purple bruise had formed along his jaw. "What is the point?"

I hesitated, not sure how to explain. "No one likes being told their life won't mean anything. We're all scared enough that'll happen already."

"Not you," Tomas said.

"Why not me?" I jumped down from the desk. "Why

shouldn't I be scared? Tomas, haven't you ever been afraid of failing at anything?"

"No." He said it so calmly I almost believed him.

"Not until six months ago, anyway."

I whirled around to see who'd spoken. Someone stood in the doorway, a suitcase on the floor beside him. He wore jeans and a T-shirt, but the outfit didn't look right. The sneakers were too clean and neatly laced, the jeans dyed too deep a blue. The T-shirt was stiff and unwrinkled, as if someone had ironed it. He looked like he was trying hard to fit in, but failing because he put so much work into it.

"Who are you?" I wondered how long he'd been standing there.

The boy ran a hand through his thin brown hair. He wasn't nearly as cute as Tomas. His eyes were blue, but they lacked Tomas's intensity. Everything about him was mellow—his loose shoulders, the way he shoved his hands into his pockets. He was much too relaxed for the clothes he wore—and the result was that you forgot about the clothes, after a moment or two.

"I'm Tomas Alvarov," the boy said. He almost sounded embarrassed. "And he isn't."

For a moment it didn't quite sink in. Then I turned to face Tomas—the Tomas I thought I knew, the one with blond hair—and waited for him to deny the boy's words. He avoided my eyes. His hands were clenched into tight fists.

"Who are you?" I finally asked.

"Steven. Steven Archer." His gaze dropped to the floor.

"He couldn't handle losing," the boy said.

"Losing what?" I stared at them both.

Tomas—no, Steven, that was his real name—shifted uneasily. "There was an essay contest. To decide who would get to come back."

"Not just an essay," the real Tomas said. "Lots of other stuff, too. Interviews, and acting things out. I was sure Steve would win—everyone was. But they chose me." The boy shrugged. "I think it's the first time in his life Steve ever lost anything."

I could fill in the rest of the story on my own. "You snuck through, didn't you?" I glared at Steven. He'd tricked me, me and all the other kids. No wonder he'd dressed wrong and hadn't understood so many other things. The Institute had never explained anything to him, because he wasn't supposed to be here in the first place.

"There was a technical problem," Steven said. "The sendoff got delayed. By the time they were ready to go, the techs were so worried about getting Tomas out before the window closed that they didn't pay much attention. Since I'd gotten through security, they assumed I was legit."

I wondered how the hell Steven had gotten through security in the first place. I decided not to ask.

"You knew they'd switch us as soon as the next window opened," Tomas said.

"One day was better than nothing." Steven's voice turned suddenly smug. "Besides, I got to meet her." He pointed at me. I looked away. My stomach felt funny when he talked about me like that.

"I bet you won't even figure out who she is," Steven said. "Of course, you wouldn't let on, even if you did.

I'm sure the Institute trained you well. You won't make any stupid mistakes, like wearing the wrong clothes, or expecting everyone to have a car, or—" A strange, bitter look crossed his face. "Or telling someone that they might be important one day."

Tomas opened his mouth to say something, but Steven cut him off. "The Institute people are waiting for me outside, right?"

"They're talking to your teachers. Explaining that they sent us to the wrong schools. You probably won't get into trouble until you go back home."

"No," Steven's voice dripped sarcasm, "I probably won't." He stood, nodded at me, and walked across the room. He brushed past Tomas, into the hall.

For a moment I just stared after him. Then I realized he was leaving, and I took off at a run. If he left, I'd never find out. Not for fifty years. My heart began to pound. My footsteps echoed down the hall.

"You have to tell me!" I grabbed Steven's arm. I knew I was breaking my word, but I didn't have any choice. He was leaving. I wouldn't get another chance.

"I can't." There was real regret in Steven's voice. "Your mom was right. It was just another one of my stupid mistakes. I shouldn't have said anything at all."

"It's not fair." My voice wavered between anger and tears. "It's not fair to just hint at my future, then leave without telling me the rest."

Steven shrugged. "Lots of things aren't fair."

I searched for some argument that might change his mind. "You're in trouble anyway, aren't you? Telling me couldn't make things all that much worse."

An ironic smile crossed Steven's face. "Only if they

found out." And then, "I should have won. I don't know why they chose Tomas. Everyone knew I was more qualified. It's just that damn Institute—"

No, I thought, it wasn't the Institute. It was that Steven couldn't handle the thought that he might not be so smart after all.

"Will you tell me?" I asked.

For a moment, he hesitated. Then his face broke into a grin. "Kimberly Susan Wilkins," he said slowly, "is going to discover time travel."

"What?" I just stared at him.

"And now that I've told you, you'd better not screw it up. Or else we'll both be in trouble." Steven started walking again.

I called after him, but this time he wouldn't turn around. Time travel, I thought numbly. How the hell was I supposed to do that? I wasn't even passing math.

Maybe Steven had made it up, as a way to avoid telling me the truth. Maybe it was just some sort of joke. A trick, like his coming here in the first place had been a trick. Maybe he didn't know my future any better than Krista's.

Then again, maybe he did. There was no way to know.

I walked slowly back to the classroom. Tomas Alvarov still sat there, slouched in one of the chairs. "I'm sorry about the confusion," he said. "The Institute will explain to your mother and the principal. Everyone else will think the Arakistanians just made a mistake and switched their students."

I nodded, only half listening. "Tomas," I asked,

"What does the name Kimberly Susan Wilkins mean to you?"

"Who?" Tomas shrugged, so casual I almost believed he didn't know.

Almost. Something—a tightness in his face, a slight clenching of his jaw—gave him away. That's when I knew Steven hadn't made anything up. I was going to discover time travel. I really was.

A cold lump settled in my stomach. For just a moment, I wished I were like Krista, or the other kids in the cafeteria. I wished I didn't know what was going to happen. What if I still messed up somehow?

A bell rang; footsteps and voices filled the hall. Tomas stood, and together we left the room.

Just outside the doorway, I turned and stared at him. Tomas stared back. His face was open, friendly. He didn't speak, just waited for me to start walking again. Steven was right. The Institute had trained Tomas well. He wouldn't give anything else away.

If I was going to discover time travel, I'd have to do it on my own.

Jane Yolen

WILDING

Zena bounced down the brownstone steps two at a time, her face powdered a light green. It was the latest color and though she didn't think she looked particularly good in it, all the girls were wearing it. Her nails were striped the same hue. She had good nails.

"Zen!" her mother called out the window. "Where are you going? Have you finished your homework?"

"Yes, Mom," Zena said

without turning around. "I finished." *Well, almost,* she thought.

"And where are you—"

This time Zena turned. "Out!"

"Out where?"

Ever since Mom had separated from her third pairing, she had been overzealous in her questioning. *"Where are you going? What are you doing? Who's going with you?"* Zena hated all the questions, hated the old nicknames. Zen. Princess. Little Bit.

"Just out."

"Princess, just tell me where. So I won't have to worry."

"We're just going Wilding," Zena said, begrudging each syllable.

"I wish you wouldn't. That's the third time this month. It's not . . . not good. It's dangerous. There have been . . . deaths."

"That's gus, Mom. As in bo-gus. Ganda. As in propganda. And you know it."

"It was on the news."

Zena made a face but didn't deign to answer. Everyone knew the news was not to be trusted.

"Don't forget your collar, then."

Zena pulled the collar out of her coat pocket and held it up above her head as she went down the last of the steps. She waggled it at the window. *That,* she thought, *should quiet Mom's nagging.* Not that she planned to wear the collar. Collars were for little kids out on their first Wildings. Or for tourist woggers. What did she need with one? She was already sixteen and, as the Pack's song went:

Sweet sixteen
Powdered green
Out in the park
Well after dark,
Wilding!

The torpedo train growled its way uptown and Zena stood, legs wide apart, disdaining the handgrips. *Hangers are for tourist woggers,* she thought, watching as a pair of high-heeled out-of-towners clutched the overhead straps so tightly their hands turned white from blood loss.

The numbers flashed by—72, 85, 96. She bent her knees and straightened just in time for the torp to jar to a stop and disgorge its passengers. The woggers, hand-combing their dye jobs, got off, too. Zena refused to look at them but guessed they were going where she was going—to the Entrance.

Central Park's walls were now seventeen feet high and topped with electronic mesh. There were only two entrances, built when Wilding became legal. The Westside Entrance was for going in. The 59th Eastside was for going out.

As she came up the steps into the pearly evening light, Zena blinked. First Church was gleaming white and the incised letters on its facade were the only reminder of its religious past. The banners now hanging from its door proclaimed WILD WOOD CENTRAL, and the fluttering wolf and tiger flags, symbols of extinct mammals, gave a fair indication of the wind. Right now wind meant little to her, but once she was Wilding, she would know every nuance of it.

Zena sniffed the air. Good wind meant good tracking. *If* she went predator. She smiled in anticipation.

Behind her she could hear the tip-taps of wogger high heels. The woggers were giggling, a little scared. *Well,* Zena thought, *they should be a little scared. Wilding is a pure New York sport. No mushy woggers need apply.*

She stepped quickly up the marble steps and entered the mammoth hall.

PRINT HERE, sang out the first display. Zena put her hand on the screen and it read her quickly. She knew she didn't have to worry. Her record was clear—no drugs, no drags. And her mom kept her creddies high enough. Not like some kids who got turned back everywhere, even off the torp trains. And the third time, a dark black line got printed across their palms. A month's worth of indelible ink. *Indelis* meant a month full of no: no vids, no torp trains, no boo-ti-ques for clothes. And no Wilding. *How,* Zena wondered, *could they stand it?*

Nick was waiting by the Wild Wood Central outdoor. He was talking to Marnie and a good-looking dark-haired guy who Marnie was leaning against familiarly.

"Whizzard!" Nick called out when he saw Zena, and she almost blushed under the green powder. Just the one word, said with appreciation, but otherwise he didn't blink a lash. Zena liked that about Nick. There was something coolish, something even statue about him. And something dangerous, too, even outside the Park, outside of Wilding. It was why they were seeing each other, even after three months, though Zena had never, would never, bring him home to meet her mother.

That dangerousness. Zena had it, too.

She went over and started to apologize for being late, saw the shuttered look in Nick's eyes, and changed her apology into an amusing story about her mom instead. She remembered Nick had once said *"Apologies are for woggers and kids."*

From her leaning position, Marnie introduced the dark-haired guy as Lazlo. He had dark eyes, too, the rims slightly yellow, which gave him a disquieting appearance. He grunted a hello.

Zena nodded. To do more would have been uncoolish.

"Like the mean green," Marnie said. "Looks coolish on you, foolish on me."

"Na-na," Zena answered, which was what she was supposed to answer. And, actually, she did think Marnie looked good in the green.

"Then let's go Wilding," Marnie said, putting on her collar.

Nick sniffed disdainfully, but he turned toward the door.

The four of them walked out through the tunnel, Marnie and Lazlo holding hands, even though Zena knew he was a just-met. She and Marnie knew everything about one another, had since preschool. Still, that was just like Marnie, overeager in everything.

Nick walked along in his low, slow, almost boneless way that made Zena want to sigh out loud, but she didn't. Soundless, she strode along by his side, their shoulders almost—but not quite—touching. The small bit of air between them crackled with a hot intensity.

As they passed through the first set of rays, a dull yellow light bathed their faces. Zena felt the first shudder go through her body but she worked to control it. In front of her, Lazlo's whole frame seemed to shake.

"Virg," Nick whispered to her, meaning it was Lazlo's first time out Wilding.

Zena was surprised. "True?" she asked.

"He's from O-Hi," Nick said. Then, almost as an afterthought, added, "My cousin."

"O-Hi?" Zena said, smothering both the surprise in her voice and the desire to giggle. Neither would have been coolish. She hadn't known Nick had any cousins, let alone from O-Hi—the boons, the breads of America. No one left O-Hi except as a tourist. And woggers just didn't look like Lazlo. Nick must have dressed him, must have lent him clothes, must have cut his hair in its fine duo-bop, one side long to the shoulder, one side shaved clean. Zena wondered if Marnie knew Lazlo was from O-Hi. Or if she cared. *Maybe,* Zena thought suddenly, *maybe I don't know Marnie as well as I thought I did.*

They passed the second set of rays; the light was blood red. She felt the beginnings of the change. It was not exactly unpleasant, either. *Something to do,* she remembered from the Wilding brochures she had read back when she was a kid, *with manipulating the basic DNA for a couple of hours.* She'd never really understood that sort of thing. That reminded her of the first time she'd come to Wild Wood Central, with a bunch of her girlfriends. Not coolish, of course, just giggly girls. None of them had stayed past dark and none had been greatly changed that time. Just a bit of hair, a bit of fang. Only Ginger had gotten a tail. But then she was the only one who'd hit puberty, early; it ran in Ginger's family. They'd all gone screaming through the Park as fast as they could and they'd all been wearing collars. Collars made the transition back to human easy, needing no effort on their parts, no will.

Zena reached into the pocket of her coat, fingering the leather collar there. She had plenty of will without it. *Plenty of won't, too!* she thought, feeling a bubble of amusement rise inside. *Will/won't. Will/won't.* The sound bumped about in her head.

When they passed the third rays, the deep green ones, which made her green face powder sparkle and spread in a mask, Zena laughed out loud. Green rays always seemed to tickle her. Her laugh was high, uncontrolled. Marnie was laughing as well, chattering almost. The green rays took her that way, too. But the boys both gave deep, dark grunts. Lazlo sounded just like Nick.

The brown rays caught them all in the middle of changing and—too late—Zena thought about the collar again. Marnie was wearing hers, and Lazlo his. When she turned to check on Nick, all she saw was a flash of yellow teeth and yellow eyes. For some reason, that so frightened her, she skittered collarless through the tunnel ahead of them all and was gone, Wilding.

The park was a dark, trembling, mysterious green; a pulsating, moist jungle where leaves large as platters reached out with their bitter, prickly auricles. Monkshood and stagbush, sticklewort and sumac stung Zena's legs as she ran twisting and turning along the pathways, heading toward the open meadow and the fading light, her new tail curled up over her back.

She thought she heard her name being called, but when she turned her head to call back, the only sounds out of her mouth were the pipings and chitterings of a beast. Still, the collar had been in her pocket, and the clothes, molded into monkey skin, remained close enough to her to lend her some human memories. Not as strong as if she had been collared, but strong enough.

She forced herself to stop running, forced herself back to a kind of calm. She could feel her human instincts fighting with her monkey memories. The monkey self—not predator but prey—screamed, *Hide! Run! Hide!* The human self reminded her that it was all a game, all in fun.

She trotted toward the meadow, safe in the knowledge that the creepier animals favored the moist, dark tunnel-like passages under the heavy canopy of leaves.

However, by the time she got to the meadow, scampering the last hundred yards on all fours, the daylight was nearly gone. It was, after all, past seven. Maybe even close to eight. It was difficult to tell time in the park.

There was one slim whitish tree at the edge of the meadow. *Birch,* her human self named it. She climbed it quickly, monkey fingers lending her speed and agility. Near the top, where the tree got bendy, she stopped to scan the meadow. It was aboil with creatures, some partly human, some purely beast. Occasionally one would leap high above the long grass, screeching. It was unclear from the sound whether it was a scream of fear or laughter.

And then she stopped thinking human thoughts at all, surrendering entirely to the Wilding. Smells assaulted her—the sharp tang of leaves, the mustier trunk smell, a sweet larva scent. Her long fingers tore at the bark, uncovering a scramble of beetles. She plucked them up, crammed them into her mouth, tasting the gingery snap of the shells.

A howl beneath the tree made her shiver. She stared down into a black mouth filled with yellow teeth.

"Hunger! Hunger!" howled the mouth.

She scrambled higher up into the tree, which began to shake dangerously and bend with her weight. Above, a pale, thin moon was rising. She reached one hand up, tried to pluck the moon as if it were a piece of fruit, using her tail for balance. When her fingers closed on nothing, she chittered unhappily. By her third attempt she was tired of the game and, seeing no danger lingering at the tree's base, climbed down.

The meadow grass was high, and tickled as she ran. Near her, others were scampering, but none reeked of predator and she moved rapidly alongside them, all heading in one direction—toward the smell of water.

The water was in a murky stream. Reaching it, she bent over and drank directly, lapping and sipping in equal measure. The water was cold and sour with urine. She spit it out and looked up. On the other side of the stream was a small copse of trees.

Trees! sang out her monkey mind.

However, she would not wade through the water. Finding a series of rocks, she jumped eagerly stone-to-stone-to-stone. When she got to the other side, she shook her hands and feet vigorously, then gave her tail a shake as well. She did not like the feel of the water. When she was dry enough, she headed for the trees.

At the foot of one tree was a body, human, but crumpled as if it were a pile of old clothes. Green face paint mixed with blood. She touched the leg, then the shoulder, and whimpered. A name came to her. *Marnie?* Then it faded. She touched the unfamiliar face. It was still warm, blood still flowing. Somewhere in the back part of her mind, the human part, she knew she should be doing something. But *what* seemed muddled and far away. She sat by the side of the body, shivering uncontrollably, will-less.

Suddenly there was a deep, low growl behind her and she leapt up, all unthinking, and headed toward the tree. Something caught her tail and pulled. She screamed, high, piercing. And then knifing through her mind, sharp and keen, was a human thought. *Fight.* She turned and kicked out at whatever had hold of her.

All she could see was a dark face with a wide hole for a mouth, and staring blue eyes. Then the creature was on top of her and all her kicking did not seem to be able to stop it at all.

The black face was so close she could smell its breath, hot and carnal. With one final human effort, she reached up to scratch the face and was startled because it did not feel at all like flesh. *Mask,* her human mind said, and then all her human senses flooded back. The Park was suddenly less close, less alive. Sounds once so clear were muddied. Smells faded. But she knew what to do about her attacker. She ripped the mask from his face.

He blinked his blue eyes in surprise, his pale face splotchy with anger. For a moment he was stunned, watching her change beneath him, no longer a monkey, now a strong girl. A strong, screaming girl. She kicked again, straight up.

This time he was the one to scream.

It was the screaming, not the kicking, that saved her. Suddenly there were a half-dozen men in camouflage around her. Men—not animals. She could scarcely understand where they'd come from. But they grabbed her attacker and carried him off. Only two of them stayed with her until the ambulance arrived.

"I don't get it," Zena said when at last she could sit up in the hospital bed. She ached everywhere, but she was alive.

"Without your collar," the man by her bedside said, "it's almost impossible to flash back to being human. You'd normally have to wait out the entire five hours of Wilding. No shortcuts back."

"I know that," Zena said. It came out sharper than she meant, so she added, "I know you, too. You were one of my . . . rescuers."

He nodded. "You were lucky. Usually only the dead flash back that fast."

"So that's what happened to that . . ."

"Her name was Sandra Maharish."

"Oh."

"She'd been foolish enough to leave off her collar, too. Only she hadn't the will you have, the will to flash and fight. It's what saved you."

Zena's mind went, *Will/won't. Will/won't.*

"What?" the man asked. Evidently she had said it aloud.

"Will," Zena whispered. "Only I didn't save me. You did."

"No, Zena, we could never have gotten to you in time if you hadn't screamed. Without the collar, Wild Woods Central can't track you. He counted on that."

"Track me?" Zena, unthinking, put a hand to her neck, found a bandage there.

"We try to keep a careful accounting of everything that goes on in the park," the man said. He looked, Zena thought, pretty coolish in his camouflage. Interesting looking, too, his face all planes and angles, with a wild brushy orange mustache. Almost like one of those old pirates.

"Why?" she asked.

"Now that the city is safe everywhere else, people go Wilding just to feel that little shiver of fear. Just to get in touch with their primal selves."

" 'Mime the prime,' " Zena said, remembering one of the old commercials.

"Exactly." He smiled. It was a very coolish smile. "And it's our job to make that fear safe. Control the chaos. Keep prime time clean."

"Then that guy . . ." Zena began, shuddering as she recalled the black mask, the hands around her neck.

"He'd actually killed three other girls, the Maharish girl being his latest. All girls without their collars who didn't have the human fight-back know-how. He'd gotten in unchanged through one of the old tunnels which we should have had blocked. *'Those wild girls,'* he called them. Thanks to you, we caught him."

"Are you a cop?" Zena wrinkled her nose a bit.

"Nope. I'm a Max," he said, giving her a long, slow wink.

"A Max?"

"We control the Wild Things!" When she looked blank, he said, "It's an old story." He handed her a card. "In case you want to know more."

Zena looked at the card. It was embellished with holograms, front and back, of extinct animals. His name, Carl Barkham, was emblazoned in red across the elephant.

Just then her mother came in. Barkham greeted her with a mock salute and left. He walked down the hall with a deliberate, rangy stride that made him look, Zena thought, a lot like a powerful animal. A lion. Or a tiger.

"Princess!" her mother cried. "I came as soon as I heard."

"I'm fine, Mom," Zena said, not even wincing at the old nickname.

Behind her were Marnie, Lazlo, and Nick. They stood silently by the bed. At last Nick whispered, "You okay?" Somehow he seemed small, young, boneless. He was glancing nervously at Zena, at her mother, then back again. It was very uncoolish.

"I'm fine," Zena said. "Just a little achey." If Barkham was a tiger, then Nick was a cub. "But I realize now that going collarless was really dumb. I was just plain lucky."

"Coolish," Nick said.

But it wasn't. The Max was coolish. Nick was just . . . just . . . foolish.

"I'm ready to go home, Mom," Zena said. "I've got a lot of homework."

"Homework?" The word fell out of Nick's mouth.

She smiled pityingly at him, put her feet over the side of the bed, and stood. "I've got a lot of studying to do if I want to become a Max."

"What's a Max?" All four of them asked at once.

"Someone who tames the Wild Things," she said. "It's an old story. Come on, Mom. I'm starving. Got anything still hot for dinner?"

JOY OESTREICHER

VET-O-SAURUS

"The thing is," Ntamba said, "nobody's communicating."

"Uh-huh," I said back to him, and turned to slap the drawer closed on my truly ancient—I mean, fully old, old, *old!*—CD player. My whole system rocked from my drawer slamming.

I propped my feet back up on my desk, nudging the equipment for my chemistry experiment out of the way.

Apiary Sneeze blasted out

of the speakers with a fully satisfactory beat, but it washed out whatever Ntamba said next. Shaking my shoulders in time to the Sneeze, I raised a hand to Ntamba. "Hey, wait," I told him. "Back up. Restart."

"Jeez, China. If you'd turn down the volume—!"

I made a move like I would activate the horrible old holocube I keep to discourage salesmen who call. The cube is an ad for kids' cereal, with cute little dancing elves and stuff, and Ntamba truly hates it. He flinched satisfactorily, and I grinned. I did turn the volume down, to help us communicate better. Then Ezra, my pet lizard, ran up my leg. I lifted him up and set him on my head, where he likes to hide in my hair and watch everything.

"Hey," Ntamba said. "You want to know why I called, or not?"

"Uh, to find out the requirements for our mechanics project? No. Maybe 'cause you're next on the list for the chemistry gear after me? Nope. Hmm." I rubbed my forehead.

Ntamba leaned toward his camera, filling the view. "Because," he shouted, "they're going to recall the dragons!"

I sat up. My feet dropped to the floor and I faced my holocam dead-on. "What?"

"Dear Ms. Future-Vet-o-Sarus, your career is on the line. Your job-to-be won't exist if the saurians all go extinct again." It was Ntamba's turn to sit down and prop up his feet. He was spectrally smug about being accepted into med school. There were still plenty of *people* who got sick.

Well, hey, even if they got rid of dragons, it wouldn't mean *all* the saurians would go. I could still be a veterinarian, specializing in the *other* resurrected species. But—no dragons? I leaned back and cut off the CD. With me, there's a dragon priority, even over my favorite boshband.

"Why a dragon recall?" I said, studying Ntamba's ebony face. He wasn't fooling me; this was serious.

"When we all had our community meeting to decide where to place the dragons' nest . . . ?"

Ezra's tiny claws patted my scalp as I nodded again.

"Nobody talked to the farmers." Ntamba shook his head. "Turns out dragons lust for bandova fruit. Fully, spectrally, lust for it."

I called up my ecology text, and then my biology index, and finally my unabridged dictionary in order to find out what, exactly, bandova fruit are. Turns out they're originally from South America—a fancy designer fruit that grows well in our climate, too.

Then I checked the Committee to Reintroduce Dinosaurs research. They had made sure the nest was placed where dragons wouldn't dive-bomb truckers on the interstate (that kept the mechanicos happy), where they wouldn't nest on rooftops or poop in the parks (keeping the Town Council smiling), and where they wouldn't introduce contaminants into biolabs and electronics manufactories.

Everybody happy? Not so.

Ntamba was right about the farmers—there weren't any on the Committee. But he was wrong about talking to them—according to public records, the local Grange *had* been consulted, and nobody'd had a problem with putting a dragon nest up in the crags overlooking the Pacific—then. Now they were complaining to the news-links and cursing the Committee because of dragon raids on their fields.

Who would have guessed that dragons have a sweet tooth for fancy fruit?

"So, Dad, it's kind of my problem, now." I unwrapped the hot *vejitos* and put two on each plate. "Of all the reintroduced dinosaurs, the dragons are my favorite."

"Not real," Dad said around a mouthful of *vejito*. Steam came out between his lips as he talked. He huffed and fanned his mouth. "Hot!"

"Well, hey, they just came out of the microwave. What's not real?"

Could have been Dad who's not real. He's an entertainment designer. This means his mind has to be . . . uh, sort of *skewed*. Like, spectrally creative. He's kind of retro, too, and a major packrat. Our loft looks like an art-junk warehouse. That's where I got my CD player and lots of other stuff. I'm told my mom couldn't deal with all that, so she left. She's a big-time computer whiz in the city, now, as weird in her own way as Dad is.

See, I can never tell what Dad will come up with. Sometimes his creativity gets applied perfectly to problem solving. He designs something, maybe he even builds it, and it works. At other times, he's utterly useless. He gets ideas that are just crazy.

"*Dragons* aren't real," he said now, answering my question. "That is," he spoke distinctly, with his mouth empty, "they are not a re-creation of anything that was a real dinosaur, unlike the other reintroduced ones." He took another bite.

"Yeah, I know they adapted them, because the pterosaurs were only gliders, and most of them weren't that big."

"And your dragons nest on the ground, and they can walk. Pterosaurs barely shuffled along. Tiny feet. Weak legs."

"They based them on *Rhamphorhynchus,*" I said, "adding bellows and an inflatable body so they could lift off the ground, not just glide out from heights."

"Well, they're based on pterodactyls, too," Dad said. "It's still a mystery how *those* things got airborne. Anyway, the dragons come more from medieval fantasy than from anything that really lived."

"They're still animals who need veterinary care, and they're still my favorites."

Dad got that glazed, creative look in his eyes. "Unh," he said unhelpfully. He stuck the rest of his second *vejito* in his pocket and turned to his synthesizer console.

I would have to investigate further. Books. Logic. Exploratory missions.

I took the bus to visit my schoolmate Ian. His farm was one of the primary sites of the dragon raids—on the coast road, between our village and the dragons' nest. We don't meet very often—school doesn't, I mean—but there are some things that have to be done in person (and besides, it's part of proper socialization training)—so I knew Ian, vaguely. Like me and Ntamba, he took a lot of chemistry and biosciences, ecology and stuff. Like me, he was concerned about dragons and bandova fruit. We were sort of on opposite sides of the thing, though. It was the bandova fruit *he* wanted to save.

We stood staring at the swath of destruction the dragon family had made in Ian's family's fields.

"They squash as many as they eat," Ian said, pointing to the smashed golden fruit. He scowled. "And their claws poke holes in the ones they don't squash."

"Well, maybe we could make, like, scaredragons."

He gave me a look like I'd just fallen out of the recycling bins.

"You know," I explained. "Like scarecrows, to keep the crows out of the corn." I'd done my research.

"Those things never worked," Ian said. He shook his head in disgust.

Maybe I hadn't done research *enough*. I didn't have any other ideas, though, so I shrugged.

"Anyway"—Ian's voice dripped contempt—"dragons are 'way smarter than crows, that's why they're such a problem. We put in nets, all across the fields, to camouflage the fruit, and to keep dragons from landing . . ."

"Yeah?"

"Well, they just get one of the biggest dragons to pick up an edge of the net. He holds it in his feet and flies down the rows, uncovering the fruit. Then they all land and have their picnic."

Did they put the net back when they were done? I wondered but, looking at Ian's humorless face, didn't ask. "What about staking the nets down or weighting them, like with I-beams?"

"Then *we* can't get to the fields either."

Hmm. That would be a problem. "How about radio collars?"

Ian's uptilted eyes squinted at me.

"Like for people's pet dogs. They deliver a mild shock if the animal goes where it isn't supposed to. The shock can get stronger as they get closer to the forbidden fence, or whatever." It discourages them without hurting them.

"Huh," Ian said. "But then you need a generator or something in the collars, and sensors all over the fields."

"Batteries run the collar. Of course, they'd have to be adjusted—made bigger for dragons. Then a sensor fence around the perimeter . . ."

"That'd be fine if they only came across the edges, but they can—"

"Drop down out of the sky. You're right. You'd have to put sensors all over the fields."

"Might work," he said. "Who's paying for 'em?"

Obviously not the farmers. I sighed.

My allowance would cover about one collar a month. And that didn't even count the sensors, of which we needed a hundred or so. The local Committee wasn't going to throw good money after bad, that was sure. No matter how scenic I thought the dragons were, there wasn't any evidence they'd drawn any tourists at all, yet. Charming, quaint, and a pain in the—

"And then somebody's got to keep changing the batteries, which means catching the dragons once every six months or whatever." Ian made a face. "And that doesn't—"

"You're right! It won't work. We need something

else." A cheap, easy-to-implement and yet safe-for-bandovas-and-dragons solution. "I'll have to think about it," I said.

"Think fast," Ian said. "My dad's getting out his pellet gun."

It was my turn to squint. What good was a pellet gun going to be against dragonhide? Except for the wings, they— Oh, wow. Of course. Mr. Farmer was going to punch holes in the delicate wings. A hole meant the entire wing surface would shred. The dragons wouldn't be able to fly, and if they couldn't fly, they couldn't eat.

I glared at Ian. That would solve their bandova problem, but it was a spectrally bad solution. "I think the SPCA might have something to say about that."

He shook his head. "Dragons aren't official animals, yet."

I'll give him credit, he didn't seem to think shooting their wings apart was a swell idea. I mean, he wasn't gloating or anything. It was simply the only answer they had.

I'd just have to come up with a better one. Fast.

Ntamba wasn't any help, but then, he wasn't very motivated. He's not even that fond of Ezra, much less the dragons. Besides, *his* job future was secure.

I couldn't think of anything. I didn't find anything helpful in any of my texts, encyclopedias, or other resources. Ezra just stared at me, his little lizard face all greeny-brown and silent.

"Dad, I need your help," I said. "I mean, like, creative ideas, problem-solving-type help."

"Find out what they're afraid of," he said.

"Ian says scaredragons won't work."

"How does he know?" Dad wondered, with impeccable logic.

I smacked myself in the forehead. *Ian doesn't know any more about dragons than I do!* "Jeez. And I was fully listening to him! Thanks, Dad."

"No soap . . . *radio!*" my dad said, laughing maniacally.

I didn't think he meant that as a clue, so as he turned back to his synthesizer boards, I left to do some on-site dragon research.

The stupid bus turns around at the last farm—'way past Ian's but 'way before the end of the road—so I took along Dad's little fold-up bicycle he used when he commuted to the city. He'd take the bus through the suburbs, then bike the rest of the way, because they don't let buses into downtown anymore. The streets really *are* swarming with bicycles, just like they show in the holos—and you can breathe the downtown air now. Mom says it's a *lot* better in the city than it used to be.

I had a nice ride on the road; it goes along the coast, and the waves were smashing against rocks and sending spray everywhere. When the road ended, I folded up the bike and leaned it against a tree. I started out at a good pace up the stony dirt path that goes up to the crags.

My pack seemed to get heavier and heavier. I was panting by the time I got to the top, so I stopped to rest. I slurped up 90 percent of my water, then went on. The path narrowed. I stood at the dragons' nest overlook.

They like fish (they aren't true vegetarians), which

is why they need to nest near the ocean. Up here they have plenty of room to dive and fly and walk around—and catch fish.

By peeking around the boulders in the overlook, I could spy on the nest among the rocks about thirty meters below. Another hundred meters or so down from there was the ocean. I could hear it rumble, but I couldn't see it.

Inside the nest were a clan of six magnificent adults, one smaller adult, and at least two dragonets. One of the little ones was so small, he must have just hatched. I thought I could make out two more eggs, but even with Dad's good binoculars it was hard to see details. The nest was messy.

I watched for a while, but I didn't learn anything I didn't already know. I needed to experiment. Try some stuff, gauge their reactions. I opened my backpack and took out my box kite. I'd put streamers of all different colors on it, because dragons are equipped with color vision. Maybe it helps them sort out different kinds of fish or something. For sure it helps them find ripe bandova fruit. So, anyway, maybe they'd react to the colors as much as to the movement of the kite.

I had some trouble getting it to fly where they could see it. I never tried to keep a kite aloft *below* me before. It would have been trivial if I'd stood on a nice long shelf about twenty meters below the nest. I moved downslope a way and dropped the kite under their noses a few times.

If they saw the darn thing, they decided to ignore it.

Maybe I'd use the kite again, but I'd have to move lower. I had to do that anyway, to try some of the other things I'd brought. I stuffed the kite into my backpack and worked my way down among the rocks.

In the labs, the dragons are very friendly, kind of like awkward overgrown puppies. They never hurt people. Their teeth can deliver a pinching bite that can break skin if they hold on long enough (they swallow their fish whole). Their claws can pierce a bandova's tender skin, their hind legs might deliver a powerful kick, but overall, they're pretty harmless. They'd never have been approved for release otherwise.

However, nobody really knew how they'd react once they'd begun reproducing in the wild. This group and one other had been released as test cases, to be observed before more were allowed. The biolab folks mostly used hang gliders and remote-controlled video to make their observations at this nest. For all I knew, the dragons might think I was a terrible threat to their hatchlings and attack me to protect them.

The truth is, they were impressively *large* up this close, so I was careful not to let them see me.

I wound up my old Walkie-Talkie-Teddy as quietly as I could and set it in the dirt. It rocked back and forth a few times, then toddled forward. About the time it got beyond the rocks, it started singing. "Hush, little baby, don't say a word, Teddy's going to show you a mockingbird." It activated its holo display, and a small mockingbird sprang to life just above Teddy's head.

Astonished, the dragons stood there and stared, blinking their big humanlike eyes. Teddy walked and sang and displayed all kinds of birds and animals, but the dragons never moved. Teddy kept on going until he ran up against one of the adult dragons' feet, where he marched in place, still singing. The dragon lowered its head, sniffed at Teddy, then very delicately hopped out of the way.

Teddy toddled on until, looking spectrally forlorn, he fell over the cliff.

Well, hey, so Walkie-Talkie-Teddies weren't going to do the job. I made a note of my results and the probable location of the Teddy litter, and pulled out my next idea.

I set my tiny portable CD player on a rock and inserted Apiary Sneeze. I set the volume way up but didn't turn it on yet. First I had to blow up the balloons.

I assembled a manlike balloon monster, turned on the music, and raised the balloon man into the air and sort of threw it over the rock. The body floated a way toward the dragons, then settled to the ground just as Sneeze got past their intro. The balloons drifted a bit on the breeze. The dragons watched carefully, tilting their heads back and forth, as if studying everything. When the music got to a (relatively) quiet part, I shot a dart.

A balloon went *pop!* and the balloon man sort of jumped in reaction just as the Sneeze saxophone wailed.

The dragons blinked. Drat them. They just sat there, their wings folded up nice and neat, and blinked.

I was so frustrated, I ran out screeching and waving my arms, my water bottle and half-open backpack clonking off me, the balloon monster bouncing away from my kicking feet, dust flying everywhere from my stomping boots.

I got knocked down by the sudden downdraft from dragon wings. *Whup! Whup! Whup-whup-flap-whupp!* When I sat up, I saw they'd all taken to the air except one adult, who stood with its wings spread out, as if to hide the two dragonets behind it. The baby dragons had buried their heads under their wings. They looked like little teal green lumps behind the hissing adult.

Spectral! I'd found something to scare them!

Oh yeah. Fully wow, China. How are you going to replicate *that* all over the bandova fields?

Once I'd done some refinement, I discovered that merely the human figure running and yelling, or waving its arms and shouting, was enough to scare the dragons. And it kept scaring them, no matter how many times I did it. I guess it was a built-in sort of stupidness, that they never learned I wasn't going to hurt them. I could walk among them as long as I moved slowly. But running and throwing my arms around and screeching was enough to make them all take off. All but the dragonets and their guard—which was fine, because the little ones wouldn't be raiding the fields for a while yet. Presumably they'd be scared by the same thing once they got big enough to fly.

But I couldn't spend the rest of my life lying in wait in the bandova fields. I didn't think I could pay anyone else to do it, either.

"It's so boring," I told Ntamba. "It's, like, exactly the kind of thing a computer can do."

"Uh-huh," Ntamba said. "Now, about this mechanics project we have to do . . ."

He didn't know it, but that's how Ntamba more or less inspired my solution. I mean, he didn't inspire me, exactly—more like nudged me in the right direction.

Ezra and I went in to talk to my dad. "I have to build a robot," I said.

"I didn't think they gave you enough parts for that," Dad said. "Aren't you supposed to just make a little mechanism?"

"Well, yeah. But to save the dragons, I need a whole robot."

"I'm sorry, China, but I don't stock robot parts."

"Well, you must have something I can use!"

"You're welcome to take anything out of the loft that doesn't have wet paint on it." None of his new stuff, he meant.

Ezra and I went upstairs. I squeezed my way past papier-mâché thingamabobs, and between cloth-wrapped wire-framed cities and, uh, landscapes, I guess you'd call 'em. I spent a lot of time scouting figurines made of various substances, because I was still thinking, *Robot, Robot.*

Ezra ran down my leg and disappeared under what looked like a gorilla that'd been Rototilled. I wandered around some more, gathering a few things that might work. On my way out, I remembered Ezra. I knelt down by the gorilla to find him.

A tornado of light flared in my face, and a hideous shrieking noise covered my own shriek as I jumped back. Heart thumping, I backed away from *it,* trying to see what it was.

After a moment, my eyes made some sense out of all that light, and I could pick out a few recognizable sounds from the wailing noise. It was *holos,* a bunch of them all playing at once, coming from behind the gorilla.

Holocubes. A gross of them or more, in a box Dad must've stuck there about a hundred years ago. Just like him to toss them aside, still in ready mode.

Ezra's little face peeped over the edge of the box, too, like he was ashamed of himself for scaring me. I scooped him up and stuck him in my hair, laughing.

Well, hey. If they scared *me,* they'd scare the *dragons,* too! I knelt again and rummaged through the box. Once in ready mode, the cubes were activated by movement: a person would walk by or wave, and the commercial would play, in full holospectric sound and color. I deactivated them all to stop the light show, then looked at them one at a time.

The first few I tried were fully as awful as my cereal elves. Awful, but not scary. Then I found her—my scaredragon. A whole series of cubes that projected a brightly dressed woman who waved her arms to show off the bracelets she was wearing. A wow boshband sound thumped beneath the voiceover. I turned up the volume and adjusted the replay speed a little so the voiceover went shrieky. The total effect was very much like a large-sized me, yelling and flailing my arms at those foolish, sweet-toothed dragons.

Fully, spectrally wow!

Ian scowled a lot while I was helping him put the cubes out among the bandova plants.

"Every time we work this field, those stupid commercials are going to play," he grumbled.

"Well, hey, it's better than squashed bandova fruit."

"My dad was going to fix that," Ian said stoutly.

"So now he won't have to."

Ian scowled some more. "Thanks," he mumbled.

I nearly dropped the box of holocubes. "Uh, it's okay. I just wanted to save the dragons."

"Me, too," Ian said, in a teeny-tiny voice.

I looked at him sideways. He looked at me sideways back, his mouth twitching into a strained sort of grin.

"Thanks, Dad. It was the perfect solution."

"You just never know what's going to come in handy," Dad said, shaking his head.

"So, about this vet-o-saurus thing," I said. "I think maybe I'll do cows, too," I said. "And horses."

"Hmm," Dad said. "I didn't think you liked things with fur."

"Well, Ian took me horseback riding, and then I got to milk a real cow. They're kind of big and soft."

Dad looked at me, an eyebrow crinkled.

"Stupid, though," I said. "Fully, spectrally stupid."

Dad nodded solemnly. Then he chuckled. "No soap . . . *radio!*" he said, and laughed out loud.

I *still* don't get it.

LAWRENCE WATT-EVANS

CELESTIAL DEBRIS

Ron checked the safety line again as he drifted smoothly along, a few centimeters from the black metal surface. Stars hung almost motionless on all sides while the metal slid swiftly beneath him.

"I wish you would use your magnetic boots," a little voice whispered in his head—the voice of the artificial intelligence he called Joey, the computer that was his constant companion and sometimes his guardian.

"Aw, Joey, they're so slow!" Ron muttered. He resented Joey's intrusion; gliding was *fun,* and it didn't hurt anyone. It wasn't as if he were playing one of his practical jokes or anything.

"But walking is much safer, and it's good exercise," Joey insisted.

"Gliding out is perfectly safe," Ron replied. "I've checked the line a million times."

"You've checked *your* end."

Ron started to reply to that, then stopped, his attention focused on a structure ahead, a large framework of piping bolted to the black metal. He was approaching the framework rapidly. He grinned. "All right, Joey," he said, "I've checked *my* end. Maybe I'll walk next time. Right now, though, it's too late; I'm here."

He straightened his legs and simultaneously reached out for the framework. His gauntleted hand closed on a pipe, bringing his glide to an abrupt halt; he swung himself around, and the magnetized soles of his heavy boots clapped onto the metal of the colony's exterior, eerily silent in the vacuum of space. He straightened up, perpendicular to the surface, as if he were standing on it, braced by the hand on the framework.

It did not *feel* as if he were standing. The colony's spin at this point on its surface was equivalent to about a quarter of a gee in the direction he had been gliding, and that meant he was hanging horizontally, face down, supported by his boots and one hand. He wasn't standing upright, no matter how it might have appeared. He was looking down through one corner of the framework into the infinite depths of empty space, with nothing below him but stars.

He was on the dark side of the colony's primary mirror, at the outer end of the great cylinder; the mirror shielded him from the glare and radiation that the Sun poured out, but he could see a narrow black sliver of Earth sliding along the rim as the colony rotated, the cities on Earth's night side a sprinkling of golden sparks.

He watched for a moment, enjoying the view. Joey reminded him, "You have only forty minutes of oxygen left."

"Oh, yeah." Joey was useful for such reminders, Ron thought. He didn't even really mind when Joey ruined some gag or other; that probably kept him out of a lot of trouble. The constant nagging about all the little stuff was tiresome, though, and when he turned sixteen one of the first things Ron intended to do was have Joey reprogrammed to eliminate all of the unnecessary fuss-budgeting.

But for now, for the next three months, he had to put up with it. Having a computer hookup inside his skull was great; having to get his parents' approval for all its programming was a pain.

He pulled his boots free and swung "down," along-side the framework of his science-fair project.

This tangle of old pipes that he had dragged out here, assembled, and mounted to the back of the mirror held the components of the project he was sure would win him the Heinlein Medal at this year's fair. He looked them over carefully.

The sensor band was still there, looped around one entire side of the structure, and the little readout at the near corner showed green. Joey agreed, "Everything is working."

The recorder also showed green, and Joey told him, "You have forty-eight hours, sixteen minutes, and thirty-five seconds of uninterrupted data flow on record, no downtime reported."

A glance at the clock readout on the upper corner of his faceplate told him that was exactly right. He nodded to himself.

The third and most essential component was also there: the huge, tapering sack that was supposed to catch anything that came through the sensor ring. But it did *not* look right. It bulged oddly at the narrow end.

Ron frowned.

His experiment was designed to collect celestial debris from the space around the colony—space garbage, cosmic junk. Space was full of dust, micrometeorites, and stray bits of this and that; he had set up his frame and giant trashbag to take advantage of the colony's spin in gathering samples of the sort of junk that constantly bombarded anything in Earth's orbit. Once he had his sample and the data from the sensors on how fast the largest pieces came in, and at what angle, he intended to analyze it all and determine how much fell into each of various categories.

In theory, he should have a few particles from the Moon, considerably more from Earth, several from elsewhere in the Solar System, and some even from outside the system entirely. He could determine how much was put there by people and how much by the rest of nature, and see how much truth there was to the accusations that humanity was cluttering up Earth's neighborhood with garbage. He could extrapolate just how much was really out there, what the chances were of eventual damage to the colony from celestial debris—oh, it would be a great entry! The judges should be very impressed.

Except that now he suspected something had gone wrong. The bulge in the collecting bag was much bigger than it should have been; forty-eight hours of normal dust accumulation shouldn't amount to more than the mass of his little finger, according to his estimates.

He must have caught something considerably larger than just a micrometeorite. That was a million-to-one chance—maybe a billion-to-one—but it looked as if it had happened.

Moving carefully, he unhooked the bag from the framework and closed it up. If he tried to look in it out here, he knew that he would probably lose half his samples, send them spinning back off into space.

When he had the bag closed, he unclipped the data recorder and stuck its Velcro backing to one of the strips on his pressure suit. Then he turned and kicked off from the nearest pipe, launching himself back toward the entryport before Joey could protest, with the collecting bag trailing along for several meters behind him.

"I really do wish you would walk," the internal computer link said.

He ignored it this time; he was too busy trying to imagine what could have happened to make that bulge in the sack.

Once he was in the airlock, instead of cycling the pumps, he fastened the mouth of the bag to the mouth of an airtight storage jar he had prepared, and then carefully poured the bag's contents into the jar.

Through the clear glass of the jar he saw a sprinkle of powder trickle in, and then a misshapen pale mass perhaps twenty centimeters long. That was obviously what had caused the bulge.

He finished emptying the bag, closed the jar, and then lifted it up to look at the object.

It was only then that he recognized it.

It was a human hand.

He almost shrieked, but he stopped himself in time and stared in horrified astonishment.

"Joey," he said, "Look at that!"

"I see it, Ron," Joey replied.

He wasn't hallucinating, then, if Joey saw it, too.

It was a man's hand, frozen solid, bloodlessly pale. The stump end was not cut or chewed but had broken off jaggedly, like a chunk of glass.

Ron knew what that meant. Someone had exposed his hand to the hard vacuum of space, and it had frozen, frozen so hard that when the man bumped it against something it had snapped right off.

And then it had gone drifting through space until Ron's collection bag had caught it.

"Oh, weird! It could have been out there for years!" he said.

"That's true," Joey said, "but I don't have any record of anyone having lost a hand in space that way, in all of recorded history, right back to the first Soviet and American flights."

"So maybe it just happened."

"I think this should be reported to the authorities immediately."

"Yeah," Ron agreed, staring at the jar.

"You have only ten minutes of oxygen left," Joey reminded him.

"Oh," Ron said. He reached for the panel and started the airlock pumps.

A few minutes later, still wearing his pressure suit but with the helmet tucked under one arm and his sample jar tucked under the other, Ron stepped into the first public vidbooth he saw, just off the main corridor outside the airlock.

His science project would have to wait; this catch was more important.

He knew who to call; his father was on the docking-port staff. He would know what to do. Ron punched in his father's code.

Instantly, the screen lit and displayed the message, CALL REFUSED.

Startled, Ron stared at that for a moment, then typed the 999 code for emergency override and hit the REDIAL button.

His father's face appeared on the screen, frowning mightily.

"Ron," he said, "I don't have any time to spare right now; we've got a man missing. This had better be serious—and unless it's *damned* serious, you had better sign off right now."

"It *is* serious, Dad!" Ron said, holding up his specimen jar. "Look what I caught."

His father blinked, and then the frown grew even more ferocious.

"It's a little early for Halloween," he said angrily.

Then he cut the connection.

"No, Dad, it's—" Ron began. Then he saw the screen go blank. "—real," he finished weakly, his shoulders slumping.

He sat there for a moment, then hit REDIAL again.

The call went through, but before Ron could say a word, his father growled, "I am *tired* of your jokes, Ron, and I am not going along with this one. You can show me your new toy later; maybe your friends will be impressed, but I'm not. I've seen fake hands before. I'm cutting off your override access for the rest of the day."

The connection broke again.

Ron stared at the blank screen for a moment, then asked, "Now what?"

"I can't answer that," Joey replied.

Ron looked at the jar. "It *is* real, isn't it?"

"I think so, but I'm not sure of it."

"You won't tell Dad it's real? Couldn't you *make* him listen?"

"As a companion computer, I'm not supposed to override personal communications unless there's imminent injury to a human being."

"But Dad's not going to accept another call from me, is he?"

"It doesn't seem likely," Joey agreed. "At least, not for the duration of the emergency."

"Then I have to report it to someone else! This hand must have come from that missing man—he's still out there somewhere, and if he's still alive he's gotta be in bad shape. *You* tell someone, Joey—isn't this a case of imminent injury?"

"I am afraid I can't justify that," Joey said. "It doesn't seem likely that the person who lost this hand could still be alive, as the hand has obviously suffered the effects of exposure to vacuum. Human beings can't survive more than about one minute in hard vacuum."

"Yeah," Ron said, "but if he sealed off his suit—I mean, suits always have seals, so you can shut off any part that gets punctured. Like a tourniquet. In case there's an accident. He must have sealed off his hand, and that's how it got frozen and broke off."

"There is no evidence that the person who lost the hand you recovered was wearing a spacesuit."

Ron blinked. "Oh, but he'd *have* to be. How else could it have happened? I mean, if he were . . . If a ship got wrecked, the hand wouldn't have snapped off, would it? And there'd be other wreckage; it'd be easy to find. And Dad didn't say he had a missing *ship,* he said he had a missing *man.*" He looked at the blank vidscreen, and asked, "Hey, Joey—can you tell me anything about this missing person?"

"I'll contact the colony databanks," Joey said.

Ron waited for perhaps two seconds before Joey continued, "The man who failed to report in on schedule is Engineer Third Class Yuri Korzhenevski. He was doing satellite repair work from a one-man scooter when communication was lost. His vehicle has been recovered; it was apparently damaged by a collision with a detached fragment of the satellite Korzhenevski was assigned to repair. Korzhenevski was not aboard the scooter."

"Well then, of *course* he was in a suit!" Ron pointed out. "You can't work from a scooter without one."

The "scooters" the people of the space colonies used for short excursions were little more than platforms with attached reaction motors and communications equipment, and with assorted tie-downs for whatever equipment might be needed. They were not true ships at all and had no life-support systems; the pilots made do with spacesuits.

"Korzhenevski was wearing a spacesuit," Joey agreed—but stopped there.

Ron let out an exasperated sigh. Joey was refusing to admit that the hand *had* to have come from Korzhenevski—who *else* could it be from?

But what had happened, then?

Ron tried to puzzle it out.

The chunk of satellite must have knocked Korzhenevski off his scooter, and for some reason he hadn't been properly tethered—otherwise he would have been able to just pull himself back.

So there he'd been, adrift in space, moving steadily away from his scooter—there wasn't anything to slow him down out there, and he and his vehicle would have continued to move away from each other with exactly the velocity they'd had at the moment he lost contact with the scooter.

But he'd have been nice and secure in his suit, with hours of oxygen, and people would have come looking for him as soon as he was late reporting in. The suit radio wasn't powerful enough to reach more than a couple of kilometers, so he couldn't call for help, but all he had to do was wait until he was missed.

So how could Korzhenevski have lost a hand?

He must have taken off his glove—but why? Even if it were torn, there'd be no reason to take it off. He could seal off the cuff without taking off the glove.

He must have been trying to do *something*, but Ron didn't see what it could have been. Why would he not just drift and wait for rescue?

Maybe he didn't *dare* wait for rescue. Maybe he couldn't afford the time. If his suit had an air leak . . .

No, he'd hardly take off a glove if the problem were a shortage of air.

What else could have been so dangerous that Korzhenevski would have done something so desperate?

And how could he still be missing with everyone searching for him?

"Oh," Ron said, realization dawning.

The suit would protect a man from everything out in space—that was what it was *for*.

Everything except falling *out* of space.

Korzhenevski must have fallen off the scooter and straight toward Earth; nothing else made sense. That meant a short fall, and then burning up in the atmosphere.

That would make it *very* difficult to wait calmly for rescue. Korzhenevski had probably panicked and started doing anything he could to slow or turn his fall.

And everyone who lived up here in orbit knew how to maneuver in space. Newton's law: For every action, there is an equal and opposite reaction. If you want to go in one direction, you throw or spray something in exactly the opposite direction.

So Korzhenevski would have tried throwing things, either to slow his fall or to turn himself aside in hopes of falling into an orbit where he might survive long enough to be rescued.

And when he ran out of other things, and got desperate enough, he must have thrown his glove.

And he must have been on Earth's night side, for his hand to freeze like that. All the moisture would have boiled away into vacuum, carrying heat with it, but if he'd been in sunlight it wouldn't have frozen so completely, would it?

Ron wasn't sure, actually, but it sounded right.

He wondered what it would have felt like, and just what *had* happened. It must have been really horrible.

But he didn't know what it had been like, and imagining it didn't have anything to do with figuring out what had happened to the missing man. He tried to concentrate on that, instead.

Throwing things would have changed Korzhenevski's trajectory—that might be why the authorities were having a hard time locating him.

He couldn't have been doing much more throwing after losing his hand, though.

Ron realized he probably knew more than anyone else about what had happened to Korzhenevski, and the situation was *urgent,* even more urgent than Ron's father thought—they had to find him not just before he ran out of air, but before he fell into the atmosphere.

But who could Ron tell?

His father wouldn't listen to him, and he didn't know who else to call—but Joey might know.

"Joey?" Ron asked.

"Yes?"

"I think I know what happened to Korzhenevski." He quickly explained his theory.

When he had finished, Joey admitted, "This seems reasonable."

"Could *you* tell someone, then? They won't listen to me."

"I can inform the colony's central computer of your hypothesis," Joey said.

"Do it, please."

Joey did.

And then Ron didn't know what to do next. He'd been planning to work on his science project, but somehow he couldn't bring himself to worry about that now.

Besides, it was all messed up by Korzhenevski's hand. That would throw off all the figures if he included it, and how could he ignore it? He couldn't just take it out of the jar and pretend it had never been there; some of the particles would probably cling to it.

And besides, how could he concentrate on a science project when Korzhenevski was out there somewhere, maybe on his way to burning up?

He sat in the vidbooth for a moment, trying to think of something more he could do to help.

He was still sitting there when the screen lit up.

"Ron Kelly?" a woman's voice asked. "We understand you may have information regarding a missing person."

"Yes!" Ron said, eager to explain.

Five minutes later, following instructions, Ron handed his sample jar over to a technician in the colony's analytical laboratory.

The technician forced a smile and thanked him, and Ron said, "You might want this, too." He held out the data recorder.

"What is it?" she asked.

"It's got the record of when the . . . when *that* hit the collector, and what direction it came from, and how fast it was traveling," he explained.

"Oh," she said. She accepted the recorder, handling it carefully, and looked at him with a little more respect. "Thank you," she said. "That should help us considerably."

Then she went away. The adults had taken over, and there was nothing Ron could do but wait. He took off his pressure suit, put it away in its locker, and then puzzled over what to do next.

He couldn't work on his science project now, even if he wanted to—he'd just given away his sample jar and data record, and he couldn't do anything on the project until he got them back.

And he'd have to find some way to compensate for that hand before he could do anything on the project, anyhow.

He knew he should go home and find something else to do, but he couldn't bring himself to leave; instead he settled into a waiting room near the dock.

It seemed like hours later that he felt the vibration that meant a shuttle was leaving the colony, but when he glanced at a clock readout he saw that it was scarcely thirty minutes since he had first seen that frozen hand, there in the airlock. No shuttle was scheduled for departure then; he would never have ventured out on the mirror that close to a scheduled launch.

"What's happening, Joey?" he asked.

"The genetic structure of the hand you found has been matched against the central files," Joey told him. "It matches the records of Engineer Third Class Yuri Korzhenevski. The approach vector of the hand has been charted and projected back to an approximate intersection with a possible vector for Korzhenevski after his separation from his scooter. A shuttle will now search the area of that intersection."

"Do you think they'll find him?" Ron asked.

"I don't know," Joey said.

The computer paused for a moment, then suggested, "Perhaps you should go home now."

Ron looked around at the empty waiting room, and at the closed and sealed doors of the docking and reception areas, and agreed. "Yeah," he said, "you're right."

He was at home, lying in his own bed and doing homework over the terminal in his skull, when the first news came. Joey tagged it for him and played it back.

"In a dramatic deep-space rescue, a team from Alvarez Colony found and brought back Yuri Korzhenevski, an engineer whose scooter, fouled by celestial debris, had gone out of control," an announcer said. "Korzhenevski's location was determined with the aid of a young colony citizen whose identity has not been revealed, whose science project intercepted a fragment lost by Korzhenevski during an attempt at orbital maneuvering. Korzhenevski's condition is reported to be critical, and no estimates are being released of his chances for survival."

"But he is alive?" Ron asked.

"Apparently," Joey said.

Ron smiled at that, a big, broad smile. He might have saved a man's life. Of course, he was way behind schedule on the science project now, but it was worth it to have helped with something like this.

At dinner that evening his parents congratulated him on his part in the rescue.

"I'm sorry I cut you off," his father said.

"That's okay," Ron said. "You were busy and upset."

His father cleared his throat and changed the subject. "It looks like Korzhenevski will live," he said. "And they'll grow him a new hand; the original was too badly damaged to reattach."

Ron nodded; he was pleased to hear that Korzhenevski would be okay.

And with Korzhenevski's future out of the way, Ron considered his own.

"What did they do with my micrometeorites from the sample jar?" he asked. "Can I get them back?"

There was a moment of silence, and then his father said, "I don't know, and that's a good question. I'll check. Excuse me." He stood up and left the table.

Ron heard him punching keys and then talking quietly to someone. A moment later Dad returned and said, "I'm sorry, Ron, but they didn't know there was anything else in the jar; it was emptied, cleaned, and sterilized after they took the hand out."

"Oh," Ron said.

That was a blow. It was all very well to have saved a man's life, and he wouldn't have changed anything if he could have, but with those samples gone, so was his entire science-fair project; there wasn't time to do it over.

And he had been bragging to his friends about what a great project he had!

Well, maybe he could come up with another one, one he could do quickly . . .

An idea struck him—a wonderful, brilliant idea, a way to keep his original project from going completely to waste. It was something no one else had ever done, he was sure.

But it might not be an idea he could use.

"Say, Dad," he said, "you said they're growing Mr. Korzhenevski a new hand?"

"That's right."

"What are they going to do with the old one?"

His mother coughed and said, "Ron! What kind of a question is that?" She looked shocked.

"Well," he explained, "since my micrometeorite project is ruined, I was wondering about doing a new science-fair project on the effects of hard vacuum on soft tissue . . ."

Deborah Coates

FLYBOY

He wanted them to call him Flyboy.

He wanted to be glorious, like the cowboy jocks who flew shuttles to the orbitals.

Tomorrow he would be twelve years old. Next week he would have his chance to bid the gangs. It was his great opportunity, his ticket to security and respect and everything he'd ever wanted.

He practiced for it in front of the mirror.

"Call me Flyboy," he said with his head cocked to one side and his eyes squinched shut as if against the glare of a red-hot desert sun in some place he'd never been and would likely never see.

"You may call me Flyboy," he tried again, looking directly into the eye of his mirror image. He wanted his voice to be flat and perfectly cool, the way he imagined shuttle jocks talked to each other out in space.

"Hey! My name is Flyboy!" he yelled at the mirror with his arms crossed and his chin jutting out. "Hey! You better know it!" But his voice cracked whenever he yelled *Hey!* so he went back to practicing the cool voice and the cocked head and waiting for his day.

When his turn finally came, he stood straight and tall in the middle of the shattered asphalt street in the shadow of the walkways that angled overhead. "My name is Flyboy," he said. It wasn't quite how he'd meant to say it. It wasn't quite as loud or quite as strong as it had sounded in front of the mirror in his room. He couldn't help but think, though, that they'd be impressed by the name he'd chosen, impressed by its glory as it rang across the tenements.

They laughed at him.

Tall lean boys with razor-sharp haircuts, leather spark jackets, and flat-silver earrings towered over him and laughed. Even his brother laughed and looked at him with stone-cold eyes as if they'd never met before. He imagined everyone everywhere joining in the laughter, people on the street, people watching from behind tattered curtains, people on other streets, in other gangs. He even imagined bright sophisticated laughter in the Heights above the walkways.

In the middle of that laughter, in the single most horrifying moment of his life, he noticed a girl across the street leaning against a stair rail. She wore mirror-shaded sunglasses, a short jacket two sizes too big for her, and fingerless gloves. She had short dark hair and small features. She stared directly at him, and what he noticed was she wasn't laughing. As soon as she realized that he was looking at her, she turned her head and looked away.

"Flyboy." The streetleader laughed again. He seemed at least twice as tall as Flyboy, wire thin and edgy. He wore three knives that Flyboy could see. Rumor had it that he carried razors in his mouth and he cut girls' faces if he didn't like the way they kissed him. He reached out with one long finger and poked Flyboy in the chest. "Fatboy, more like."

And there it was. His name.

Flyboy became sport for gangboys then. He was less than nothing, a way for them to hone their hunting skills when they weren't shooting rockets up their noses or dreaming of the moment when they would finally have the power or the money or the guns to go above the walkways.

The first time they chased him, he'd been walking down the street, not doing *anything*. Of course, he should have known better, dopey Fatboy, less than nothing. He realized that later, when he had time to catch his breath.

They chased him up an alleyway. They chased him down a barren street where the blasted hulks of storefronts loomed like giant caves. They chased him through a forest of chromium building footings. He could hear them laughing; they called out his name and made snorting noises.

He ran like he'd never run before; he ran faster than he'd ever thought he *could* run. He knew that if they caught him he'd be dead. He knew the probe addicts would tear him to pieces with their blue-tipped fingers, the spazzed-out rocketheads would laugh while he screamed, and there would be no one there to help him. So he ran.

He slid on his knees through soggy, smelly trash heaps. He stumbled over boxes. He ran until his breath came in whooping gasps and sharp pains pierced his side. But they were always behind him. He stumbled against an alley wall, paused for half a second, and started running again.

That was when he reached the tower.

It was a rocket-spired building whose roof just brushed the walkway. It was a place the streetboys never ventured, not since Handsome Jack the Charismatic had fallen through the floor six months before, right in the middle of his oratory. Steve the Reiver, leader of the Wire Girls, claimed that she could still hear Handsome Jack on quiet nights, haranguing her as he fell forever through endless rotten floors.

Flyboy stumbled across the street just ahead of his pursuers and ran inside. While the streetboys howled in frustration, he dragged himself up the broken stairs. *Why*, he thought as he gasped for breath, *why me why me why me?*

In a room at the top of the tower, Flyboy crouched

and looked down at the street through a shattered windowpane. After a few minutes the streetboys stopped howling and drifted away to find easier pickings. Flyboy watched as working joeboys, maids, and sweepers climbed down from their days above the walkway. He watched tricked-out babes cruise for city men—and sometimes women—who had slid down to the undertown for a little nighttime adventure. Once he thought he saw the mirrorshaded girl slipping in and out of the shadows, but it was on another street and he lost sight of her before he knew for sure.

Late that night, when the streets were as empty as they would ever be, Flyboy scrounged a mattress and moved himself permanently into the tower. He sat in his room and looked out onto the street, past crumbling buildings and beyond. He wanted to shout out the window at the streetboys as they passed. He wanted to taunt them from his tower. *Fatboy, ha!* he wanted to say. *If I'm so fat how come I can climb these stairs?* He wanted them to hear his laughter. *Nyah, nyah, nyah!*

But then, as he was bringing up some blankets he had scrounged, he fell through the last step from the top, fell all the way through to his waist, and it took him half an hour to scrape free. After that he decided that he'd better just keep quiet and live in the shadows, where he belonged.

Some nights Flyboy sat on the tower roof, though it was steeply pitched and shot through with holes. If he was careful, if he moved slowly, he could reach out and touch the walkway overhead. He liked to imagine that he could actually feel the vibrations of the people as they passed by above him. He found a little platform near one corner of the roof, and from there he could watch the street and still be safe from everything down below. Usually, in the murky evening, he would see the mirrorshaded girl walking down one street and up another. Sometimes she carried packages that she passed to people with shadowed faces.

One hot muggy May night, he was sitting up on his platform, dreaming of a day when he would stand tall against the gangs, when he saw a man in the street below. He knew right away there would be trouble. He knew. He should have thought or moved or . . . something. But it was too fast. It all happened so fast.

The man wore retro-bright clothes made of a shiny synthetic material, tight pants, and knee-high boots—the latest fashions up in the city. He had a flashy platinum mechanical arm and oddly rimmed eyes that looked cybernetic. He had probably come to undertown the way they all did, for sex or drugs or outlawed VR programming. Flyboy knew that the clothes would get him in trouble. The mechanicals would get him killed. Streetboys hated mechanicals, and in undertown, streetboys got to say.

Flyboy wanted to shout down at the cityman, to warn him of the terrible danger, but even before the words formed on his lips the streetboys were on him. There were only two of them. Flyboy even knew them; they hung on the corner with their babes every night. There were just two of them. *Cityman should run.* That's what Flyboy thought. He might have had a chance if he'd run. But he didn't. He just stood there.

The taller of the two streetboys, the one with orange-blue hair and tattooed lightning bolts on his arms, said something to the man that Flyboy couldn't hear. The man backed away. The orange-blue streetboy shoved him down. Cityman scrambled up, against the wall, and put his hands up in surrender. The other streetboy stabbed him three times—one, two, three—in the stomach. Then he laughed and the two streetboys walked away.

The body lay in the street against the building for three days. Someone stole his boots almost immediately. Later, his fancy shirt and his watch and his pants disappeared. Finally, the body rovers found him naked and stripped of everything, and they carried him away.

Once upon a time, Flyboy had a family. A mother, a father even, and a brother in the gangs. Once upon a time, his mother wanted him to go to school on scholarship up in the city. She took him all the way across town when he was eight years old, took him out beyond the walkways to where he could look right up and see the sun. She walked beside him with her head high, through stark white corridors that smelled sharp and clean. He'd spent six hours going from one room to another, taking test after test, until they sent him home. He never heard a word from the testers afterward, though his mother made the long trip three more times and waited by the front doors all day long for someone to let her in.

The day Flyboy made his bid and failed to join the gang, his mother packed his things in a small brown cardboard box and put it outside the door. It was waiting for him when he got home. When BoJo Cennet failed his mother had thrown his clothes right out the window, screaming at him how he'd disgraced her and endangered her and he should have known he wasn't good enough, while he scrambled on the sidewalk to gather up his things. At least Flyboy's mom had put his stuff in a box. At least she'd done that. Flyboy had knocked on the door that afternoon, though he'd known she wouldn't answer. His parents bought protection from the Jammer Boys, who would trash them in a minute if they broke the rules. They couldn't afford to want him, Flyboy the Pariah, anymore.

Flyboy had his life figured out. He was safe in the tower. He scavenged food in the early morning, when the streets were nearly empty and the air was almost fresh, overlaid with the smell of old smoke and hot rocket fuel from the shuttleport across the causeway. He studied picture books he scrounged from city trash heaps, pictures of leafy trees and blue skies and rolling hills so real and green he thought that he should be able to reach right out and touch them. He drew maps on flattened cardboard boxes, stored dented cans of food underneath the floorboards. He knew that if he could find those trees, those soft green hills, and a sky so blue it made his head hurt, he knew the people who lived there would take one look at him and know his name.

On the night of the Fourth of July, he was sitting on his mattress studying a tattered picture book while the darkness outside was ripped apart by booming cannons and wild neon flashes. His candle guttered and almost went out. He stopped trying to look at pictures and walked over to the window. As he approached he heard sudden shouts and crazy laughter. He crouched beneath the window frame, his knees drawn up to his chest, for several minutes before he could muster the nerve to raise his head and look outside.

This was the scene:

Two streetboys, the one from before with orange-blue hair and another boy with skull and crossbones tattooed on either cheek, close-cut hair and razored teeth that looked like they'd been painted reflective silver, were standing in the middle of the street with their hands on their hips and their heads thrown back. They were laughing. *Just like jackass monkeys,* Flyboy thought, *like everything is funny just because a streetboy says so.* Light sparked off their earrings, off the neon in their jackets. On the corner stood their babes, with silicone breasts, tattooed arms, and big stuck-spray hair that swept out from their heads. *Bet they think they're something,* Flyboy thought. *Bet they think they're tricked out like the real babes upstairs in the city.*

Flyboy looked at the streetboys again. The person on the ground, he realized, the person they were laughing at, was the mirrorshaded girl. She looked up at them. She brushed dirt off her knees. She stood up. They knocked her down again and laughed even harder. Fireworks burst above them; cannons roared. Flyboy wished he hadn't even looked. He wished he'd just stayed crouched down beneath the window. In a bright flash of light the girl stood up once more, and again the streetboys knocked her down.

Flyboy closed his eyes. They probably wouldn't really hurt her, he told himself. Probably. Not really bad.

He knelt down on the dirty floor with his eyes squinched shut as tight as they would go and he told himself, *They won't hurt her, they won't hurt her, they won't hurt her, they won't.* And he tried to pretend that he couldn't, in the sudden quiet between fireworks, hear the dull thud of a heavy boot kicked into someone's side.

Flyboy knows what glory is. He's seen it in the picture books at the semester school the three weeks every year he's allowed to go. He knows that glory means that men and women stand up tall. He knows that they face danger without flinching, in sharply creased uniforms and highly polished boots that seem to glow. Glory is when your chest fills up so proud you're almost bursting with it and you know what's right, you know exactly what to do, you're strong and you're brave, and everyone loves you.

That's what glory is.

Glory doesn't consider the undertown with its sharp smelly streets and nasal rocket launchers that fry the brains of all the smart young boys and girls before they're ten. Glory doesn't understand children who have never won, who have never seen the sun rise, who have never seen the stars.

Flyboy's fingers trembled as he picked up the old camping lantern he'd unearthed in an abandoned storefront. In his other hand he clasped the Acadia Shuttle Corps lighter he'd found three weeks ago on the hot asphalt outside the landing bays. He clasped it so tightly that the cheap metal bit into his hand. He flicked it to make sure that it would light, then he thrust it into his pocket and tried to think what else he had that might possibly become a weapon.

He set two heavy books down along with the lantern as he slid around the hole in the staircase. He sat on the lowest step and strained to reach back and grab them. He almost couldn't reach that far, and for a moment he thought he would just give up. At least he'd tried to help her. At least he'd thought about it. That was something, wasn't it? And if he stayed right where he was on the steps, he wouldn't even be able to hear anything. If he stayed right there, he could pretend that no one was out on the street. He could stay there and pretend until it was all over.

A low rumble shook the tower as a shuttle left the port three blocks away. Flyboy took a deep breath, grabbed the shaky stair rail, and reached out across the emptiness. Clutching the lantern and the books against his chest, he walked down the rest of the stairs.

When he looked outside, around the edge of the burned-out doorway, he saw that the streetboys had shoved the girl up against a building. The babes weren't laughing any longer; they kept looking at their boys through slitted eyes and then away.

"I have a delivery," the girl said in a calm, even voice. Flyboy wondered if she practiced, the way he did in the mirror. "It's just medicine. They need this at the Fourth Street clinic. There's retrovirus in the Jammer houses." She seemed to stare at them, though it was hard to tell with her eyes hidden underneath her glasses. "Gangers die too, you know. It ain't just for the droners."

"Yeah, yeah, girl, keep your shirt on," the orange-blue streetboy said. Then he reached out with a gloved hand and ripped her shirt all the way down to her waist, his laugh a high-pitched giggle. "Keep your shirt on. Ha ha ha."

Flyboy fumbled with his lighter in the shadows of the doorway. His fingers shook so badly that he dropped it twice and had to search for it on his hands and knees.

The orange-blue streetboy grabbed for the girl's mirrorshaded glasses. She kicked him squarely between the legs. Everyone, including Flyboy, was so surprised that for a half second everything froze.

The girl ran.

The orange-blue streetboy lay against the wall, gasping like a dying fish. The other one, tattooed skull-and-crossbones, screamed like a wild thing and drew out a souped-up Kennet laser pistol jacked from somewhere on the upper floors. He ran into the middle of the street and activated the tracker. He had all the time in the world and he knew it. The muscles in his arms began to relax as he waited for the beacon to home in on the running girl's back so he could fire.

Flyboy ran out of the shadows. He was laughing, and he would remember that one thing specifically later, because he'd never felt less like laughing in his life. But he was. He was laughing and running, his lantern finally burning. He stopped and threw it as hard as he could. It smashed on the broken street, kerosene splattered, and the streetboy's pants caught on fire. With a howl, he dropped the gun and started beating at his leg to put the fire out.

Flyboy ran away so fast he thought he might just take right off and fly. He'd done it. He had. He had he had he had he had he had. Just once, he'd done it right.

Several hours later, as he snuck through pitch black alleys to the tower, he hardly noticed that the fireworks had died and that the cannons no longer fired. He didn't pay attention to the nearly empty streets, to the hurried whispers from the shadows, or to the hidden faces in the alleys. He kept his head down and shuffled without looking where he was going. Once the euphoria was gone, he realized precisely what he had done. He'd attacked a streetboy. And they'd know it had been him. They would never let him get away, not even if it took forever. The worst part was, he'd hardly done anything. Anyone could have done what he did. He hadn't even changed the world.

The raid started just as he reached the tower. Sirens screamed. Strobe lights flashed. Armored cops dropped through security access shafts in well-armed squads of four or five. All the city's dirt was buried in the undertown—drugs and sex and VR death—and sometimes the city had to pretend it was too clean to want them.

Flyboy crept inside the tower and hauled himself carefully up the stairs. He almost didn't notice her when he entered the room, she was sitting in the corner so quietly. Then she stood and he could see her face and her mirrorshaded glasses clearly in reflected street light from a walkway overhead. She looked at him for a minute. "I've been waiting for you," she said. Flyboy pressed his back tightly against the rough unplastered wall.

She moved her hand and something glittered in her palm. She walked toward him until only inches separated them. Her glasses seemed to reflect first one color then another as the strobe lights flashed outside. Flyboy could see his face in the lenses of her glasses. He could see his wide eyes, his shock of light-colored hair with the bangs shoved up into little sweaty spikes. *What a dope you are,* he thought, and edged another step away from her.

Her hand and the glittery . . . something . . . reached out to him. He edged away. She stopped. He edged a little farther down the wall. He couldn't see her eyes through the dark glasses. He could barely see her face. He tried to flatten himself so tight against the wall that he'd just disappear.

For several minutes there was silence in the room as streetboys howled and pulse rifles flashed on the street outside. Cops shouted orders from the shadows at trackers with night sensors staked along the walkways.

Flyboy took a breath. It shuddered just a little as he let it out. "Look," he began, "Outside, before . . . I didn't mean anything. I just thought . . ."

The mirrorshaded girl shook her head, reached out again, and handed him his lighter. "You dropped this outside," she said.

Flyboy grabbed it and clutched it tightly. He hadn't even realized that it was missing. "Th-thanks," he managed to say.

"My name is Cisco." She watched him through her glasses. Then she said, "I already know your name."

Please, Flyboy pleaded silently. *Please don't don't don't don't.*

"I hear your name is Flyboy."

Flyboy.

That was what she said.

SHERWOOD SMITH

I WAS A TEENAGE SUPERHERO

The day everything started was just another hot, smoggy November day in Los Angeles. The science-fiction club and I had gone to see the latest science-fiction film, just as we always had, ever since sixth grade.

"Well, that was a rip," Jermaine glumped (as he always did) on our way out. "Those spaceships would never break atmosphere, and as for the aliens, why is it they always look like someone barfed on their faces?"

"Part of the alien myth," Jessica said, yanking open the heavy glass doors. "Like Santa and his red suit. Only, aliens have to be ugly."

I grinned to myself as I followed the others out into the hot afternoon sun. Once they'd gotten all the bad science out of their systems, they'd decide they'd liked the movie. Since I plan to be a writer, not a scientist, these things don't bother me as much.

"Extraterrestrials are myths?" Natalie asked, fanning her face with a battered Star Trek paperback as she walked next to me. "I thought a myth can't be true—like elves. There could be alien beings out there somewhere."

Noah shook his head. "There's exactly the same amount of scientific evidence for aliens as there is for elves—which is to say, none."

From Noah's other side, Marcos snorted. I looked over, saw Marcos's wheelchair, looked away again quickly in case he thought I was staring. I still had trouble trying to get my brain to put Marcos Arkardian, once the star athlete of middle school, together with my science-fiction club. Every girl at school had had a crush on him—including Yours Truly, not that he ever noticed—until he disappeared one winter, when a drunk driver had wiped out half his family and landed him in the hospital for a long stretch. After he got out he stayed away from the sports field and somehow found out about our movie club—not the book-discussion days at school. He still didn't go to school. But he came along on our Saturday movie jaunts. Not that he ever talked much, except to Noah and Jermaine.

"But there could be life on other planets!" Natalie exclaimed, her huge blue eyes bigger than ever. "We don't have any evidence that we *are* alone in the universe—"

"Of course we do," Jessica replied calmly. "No probe or signal ever sent out has gotten a response, and all we hear is noise from space—"

"I'll believe in aliens over those spaceships," Jermaine said.

"Or that fake-o ancient civilization," Noah chimed in, wiping his sweaty glasses. "Geez! Is Hollywood's idea of a convincing culture a bunch of buff people all in their twenties? I didn't count one kid—"

"Or old person," Jessica added, following the others across the street to the ice-cream store. "*Or* family."

At the doors, we paused. "Table for six is free," Jermaine said. "Marcos, it'd be a squeeze, but—"

"Gotta go," Marcos said. "Later."

"Wow, he actually spoke," I muttered behind my hand to Natalie.

"He's not a talker," she said. "But he sure reads a lot."

"How do you know?" I asked, surprised. "He's actually spoken to you? I didn't think he talked to anybody."

"Well, whenever I see him he's got at least three science-fiction books in that side pocket in his chair," she said. "Coming in?"

I looked at my watch and felt my heart start to wham.

I was actually supposed to go to my aunt's, but when Tia Nita asked me to come she'd said Top Secret.

"No," I said as casually as I could. "I, uh, have to be home."

The others went inside. Natalie didn't follow—she paused at the door, then turned and smiled at me. She was pretty and popular, but she seemed to like hanging around me—at least at school and on club days. She'd only been to my house a couple times, and I'd never been to hers.

She said, "Talked to your aunt lately? What's she's working on now?"

I shook my head, wishing I could tell her that was where I was going. Except for the club, I'd always been kind of a loner, until Natalie came to our school the year before. Kids think I'm weird because I'm interested in everything, but Nat is even *more* interested, if that's possible. "No idea," I said truthfully. "Tia Nita only talks when she's ready."

"If I had an inventor in my family, I would be over there helping every day." Natalie sighed. "Then I'd know all about her projects!"

"Yeah, well, I gotta go." I gave her a limp smile and walked away.

An hour later I sprinted up my aunt's old, cracked driveway.

"Tia Nita!" I bellowed, racing around to the side of the garage, which looked like a typical, rundown box from the outside—but inside, it was a lab straight out of Futurama. Cool air bathed my sweaty face. "I'm here! Sorry I'm late—we went to see a movie, and the bus was super slow, but here I am. Are you gonna show me your new project?"

"Hi, Mouse," Tia Nita said, setting down a small, pointy tool. "Here it is." She held up a bundle of gray cloth. "Go put this on. And—careful. That thing is worth more than my house."

I went to the little lab bathroom and struggled my way into what seemed to be some kind of padded wetsuit with ribbed joints. As small and scrawny as I am, the suit fit like a second skin. Despite the air conditioning, by the time I pulled on the flexible gloves, I was hot all over again.

I stepped out, saying, "It's real tight—and I'm about to faint, or drown in my own sweat. Is this the experiment?"

"No, *chaparracita,*" Tia Nita said with a laugh. And then: "Marcos, adjust the temp regulator before she expires."

A moment later coolness soothed me right down to my toes, but I scarcely noticed. *Marcos?*

I poked my head around a couple of file cabinets and nearly plotzed when I looked straight into those familiar eyes—dark eyes with thick lashes around them, set in a thin face with curly black hair framing it. "Uh, hi," I mumbled, feeling hot all over again. Marcos gave me a brief, absent smile, then looked away—like he was reading something important off the back of Tia Nita's T-shirt.

My aunt turned around after a silence that felt a century long and said dryly, "You two can natter about your movie later. Right now we've work to do. For which you'll be paid," she added, "so listen up."

"Energy level is low," Marcos said suddenly, frowning down at the laptop perched on a little desk across the arms of his wheelchair.

Tia Nita nodded. "Marisa, start moving—just walk back and forth, swing your arms, get used to the give-and-take of the suit."

I did, feeling even more self-conscious than before—not to mention more puzzled. Despite the suit's thickness, movement was easy—like in a leotard, not a wetsuit. And it stayed mysteriously cool inside.

"You are wearing," my aunt said, "a prototype for an antiterrorist suit. It takes kinetic energy and converts it into potential energy, then uses the stored energy to enhance your own capabilities, kind of like a self-winding watch. Hit your arm."

I smacked myself on the forearm, not hard. The suit seemed stiff for a moment, and there was no sting at all, so I smacked myself harder. Again, the suit stiffened briefly in that spot, but I felt nothing else.

She smiled approvingly. "It works kind of like a seatbelt does: You can move freely in it so long as you move normally, but a sudden impact makes it freeze. Only, here the kinetic energy does not pass into your body, but it is absorbed by the suit. It's like a giant battery and a powered exoskeleton, all in one. So when you need extra energy, the suit discharges it and you're able to move faster, and with more strength, than normal."

I tried jumping up and down, at first slowly; then I gave one big jump and almost hit the ceiling—wobbling frantically before I landed. I lost my balance and fell, but again the suit went stiff and I didn't get hurt. "Whoa!" I squawked.

Tia Nita said with a chuckle, "Your first job is to get used to the suit's limitations and capabilities, before we start field-testing it."

"Okay," I said, cautiously moving my arms.

"Now. I picked you because you're smart and you're small—I had to make every square inch of that suit myself and it took me months—and because I can trust you. No one but the three of us is to know about it. No one. *¿Sí?*"

Questions started blazing through my brain, but I shut them out. "*¡Sí!*"

"I also picked you because I know you can resist the temptation to start fights and jump buildings and punch holes through walls, which would be the first thing most people might try."

"It can do that?" I squeaked.

"If it works right, it will make you stronger and faster than the toughest man alive—and the more abuse the suit takes, the stronger you'll become. Except," she said, "keep away from scissors or knives. This is the downside of being able to move normally. There's a certain amount of protection, but I haven't figured a way to save the circuitry from slow cuts. Blows and impacts, or even a stab attempt, if it's hard enough, should be no problem. Which brings us to Marcos. He will be monitoring you on his laptop and by high-band radio—which now brings us to the helmet."

She lifted what looked like an ordinary bicyclist's helmet from her worktable and fitted it carefully over my head. "The goggles flip down and up," she said, demonstrating. Then she touched my hand. "Feel those bumps inside the fingers of your glove? Those are your lens-control buttons."

I experimented around, causing the lenses in the goggles to zoom up close to Tia Nita's face, then zoom out again. Then go blotchy and weird—

"Infrared," she said, from behind Marcos.

And I realized I was seeing heat, and tried to blink it into focus. Then I tried the last bump, which made everything crystalline clear, and kind of remote in an odd way.

"Ah, I think you've reached the best part of my system," she said. "Ever noticed how cats will focus intently on something you can't see?"

Marcos actually spoke then. "Neural clumps," he said.

"I learned about that in bio," I put in. "Different neural clumps see different things. One sees just horizontal lines, another just flowers, another just faces. Damage to that part of the brain means the person—or creature—can see everything *except* faces," I said. "As for animals, the theory is that they have neural clumps that we don't have . . ." I blinked at Tia Nita, who was grinning. "You mean, this lens adds extra neural clumps for me, is that it?"

"Those lenses don't add them, they simulate the effects—I hope," she said. "It's two lenses, alternating very quickly. I don't know what you'll see—if anything—and if you do see something, it might not be the same for anyone else. There's a current hypothesis about people in history who were considered 'fey' or 'second sighted'—you know, the ones who claimed to see ghosts or fairies. They might actually have had slightly different neural clumps than most humans, enabling them to see things that others couldn't."

"When do we get started?"

"Now," she replied with a grin, pointing to the backyard.

Well, we spent a strained hour or so experimenting with the suit. Jumping up and down was kind of fun, even when I fell. The strain was with Marcos. I tried hard not to get caught staring at him in that wheelchair. In fact, I tried so hard I managed to look everywhere else but at him when we had to talk. As for him, those superpolite "pleases" and "thank yous" made me feel like I'd gotten trapped in dancing school.

Despite the cooling system in the suit I was sweaty and hot when Tia Nita finally came out and said, "That'll do. Next I want you to test the transmit and receiver system. Timing," she added before either of us could speak, "is entirely up to you. Just report to me after you've logged twenty-five hours of testing." She turned to me. "Go ahead and wear clothes over it. The helmet shouldn't attract notice—but in case it does, remember, all it takes is one person gossiping—and I'd much rather this stayed under wraps until I am ready to go public with it."

"Oh, well, sure," I blurted. "But how about just *one* more person? She would be a big help . . ."

Tia Nita looked vaguely surprised. I snuck a glance at Marcos, but those big dark eyes were totally unreadable.

"It's my friend Natalie. She loves your work, she always talks about science, and . . . it'd mean a lot to her." *To me, too.*

"How well do you know Natalie?" Tia Nita asked. "I mean, I dislike criticizing a friend of yours, but this is important. The one time you brought your club over to see my lab, she nosed into everything. It made me uncomfortable."

I chewed my lip, thinking about Nat. "She's always that way," I said. "She's just terminally curious—like me. Heck, the first time she came to my house she messed with my miniature dollhouse collection for two hours. I don't know anything about her home life, though I think her parents must be scientists because she sure knows technical language. She just never talks about her home, but we can't hold that against her!"

Tia Nita turned to Marcos. "What do you think?"

He shrugged his thin shoulders. "I think Natalie can keep a secret."

"All right, then. One more person might be a good idea. You two handle it." She went back inside.

I turned to Marcos. "Um, what's your schedule like?"

He shrugged, his mouth twisting in an almost-smile. "Up to you."

"Shall we meet at the park tomorrow, soon's I get out of school? Or—"

"Or what?"

I glanced down, saw that chair, looked away quickly. My face felt like a ninety-hour sunburn. "Can you, um, *go* to the park?"

"Of course I can," he said. "See you there at four."

"With Nat," I reminded him.

"Right," he said, and grinned. It was an odd grin.

I sighed and got out of there fast.

First thing when I woke up, the suit—and bringing Nat in on the secret—was on my mind. As usual I raced through the shower and breakfast in order to be first at the bus stop. Being first meant I could get a good seat—no. There weren't any good seats on that ancient bus. A *safe* seat, as far away as possible from where the seniors liked to sit, especially the two overgrown boys I thought of privately as Knucklebutt and Nerd. Seemed to me their sole purpose in life was to make life miserable for smaller, younger kids (Knucklebutt) and to laugh inanely (Nerd).

Once I got to a good spot, I relaxed and thought again about the suit—and how much fun it was going to be to tell Natalie.

When the bus lurched and shuddered to a stop in front of school, Nat herself was waiting. I jumped out, opening my mouth to greet her, and was nearly flattened by a kid flying down the bus stairs right behind me. He landed on the sidewalk, his books spilling everywhere, while in the bus door Knucklebutt snickered and Nerd brayed his stupid, loud laugh.

"Stupid jerks," I muttered to Nat.

She glanced back. "Who are they?"

"Who cares?" I said. "I don't know their names and I don't want to. They're scum. Now, I've got something much better to talk about . . ." And I launched into the story of the suit. And sure enough, she was excited—asked a couple million questions. When I got to the part about the cat lenses, her eyes were really big and round.

The bell rang just then, so I said quickly, "See you at the park at four? And—promise me—it's a drop-dead secret, okay?"

She blinked. "You don't think I can keep a secret?"

"Of course!" I said hastily. "Sure! It's just, uh, a reminder."

She turned away and left with no more words. We didn't have any classes together, but we saw each other at lunch, along with the rest of the gang. Nat talked about computer stuff and books with the others like she'd never heard of any suit—or secrets.

I got to the park right at four. Marcos was waiting—and as soon as he saw me he actually spoke. "A turtleneck and sweatpants? It's ninety-five out."

"Gotta hide the suit some way." I yanked up my sleeve to show him the suit. "D'you think hockey gear would be more inconspicuous?"

He shrugged, giving me a half smile.

"Where's Nat?" I said.

He shrugged again and said, "Shall we get started?"

"Okay," I said. "If she shows up late, she can always find us."

Turning his wheelchair, Marcos headed for the little kids' area. I watched him put on his earphones, then I ran off into the thickest trees.

Before long I actually got kind of used to bouncing around and slapping at branches way overhead. I tried falls and banging into tree trunks, and as always the suit felt heavy for a moment, like a full-body cast (probably something Marcos had some experience with), then gave me even more strength. Just once I ran as hard as I could into a big tree. The suit went stiff and I felt the faintest flash of heat, then a moment of vertigo, and Marcos's voice came into my headset: "What are you doing?"

"Ran into a tree," I mumbled. "I'm okay—I think."

"Watch it. The suit will cushion your outside, but your guts still think they're going forward."

"Right," I said, jumping extra high, as if I could escape feeling like an idiot. "Whee!"

"What now?" He snorted a laugh.

"I just managed a flip over that branch way up there. Hey, this thing is more fun than a trampoline!"

"A half-a-million-buck trampoline," he said.

"Gack! Is that what Tia Nita spent on it?"

"I don't know—but the government will, if not more," he said.

I realized then that we were actually talking. "Does she tutor you? Is that how you know her?" I asked.

"Yep. She's good. I've learned more in a year from her than I did in six years of school. Not that I tried very hard in school," he added wryly. "Look. It's getting dark, and it takes me a while to get home. Let's break until tomorrow. You come by my place and we'll test the lenses."

"Okay. I just wish I could use it at school . . ." I sighed, running back through the trees toward him.

"Why?" he asked. "Kick some butt?"

"No." I laughed. "Basketball. Think how dynamite I'd be!"

"Yeah, and your aunt would have both our brains in a pickle jar."

I reached him then. He promptly shut up and started fiddling with his computer. After an awkward second or two, I just took off.

All the way home, I wondered what had happened to Natalie. Was she upset over my asking for her promise? I couldn't believe it. Had to be something else. Strict family, maybe?

As I changed out of the suit, I thought back and realized Nat had never said anything about her family. Not that this was so unusual. Since the club formed there had been two divorces and an alcohol problem among the various parents, step-parents, and half-parents. Most of the kids didn't talk about home, if they could help it.

Maybe she can't do anything after school, I thought. *Which is why we never seem to get together.*

So I got a great idea: I'd wear the suit to school—under my clothes—and find a place to test it at lunch, where no one would be able to see me but Nat.

The next morning I stared into the mirror with satisfaction. A turtleneck shirt and jeans totally covered the suit, and helmet and gloves were stashed carefully in my backpack. Unfortunately, the extra time it took to dress made me late. As I jostled my way onto the school bus, my heart sank when I saw that the only seats left were the ones nearest the Cosmic Creeps.

I leaned my head against the fingerprint-smeared window, clutching my backpack like it was a life preserver and watching the neighborhood slide by, until a sudden scream from across the aisle broke my thoughts. Knucklebutt and Nerd had gone from insulting other kids on the bus to insulting each other, which had started a wrestling match. As I looked up, one of them lunged across the aisle, grabbed a girl's binder, and conked the other guy with it. When the binder burst and papers flew everywhere, the girl screamed and the two twits just about died laughing.

So the second guy decided it was his turn, looked around and saw me, and with a nasty grin reached for my backpack.

Pure reflex made me yank it back. It snapped away from his fingers.

"Ow!" he yelled, and reached with both hands.

Thinking only of that helmet in the backpack, I swatted his hands away, then gave him a poke in the chest. Not a hard one—at least I didn't mean it to be hard—so we were both amazed when he flipped backward over the seat behind him and landed in the laps of the kids sitting there, his lanky legs kicking wildly in the air. When he managed to disentangle himself, he looked totally stunned. The entire bus rocked with laughter.

We reached school right then, and I jumped up and raced off the bus without looking at the creeps.

Nat was sitting on the bus bench, waiting. I looked around, then whispered to her, "I've got it on."

She looked startled. "All of it?"

"Well, not the helmet, of course." I patted my backpack significantly. "Anyway, let me tell you what just happened . . ." And I described the incident on the bus. At the end, I sighed and said, "It wasn't breaking my promise to my aunt, but I have to admit, it sure felt good to see that idiot flying over that seat! I hope next time he'll think twice before bullying someone smaller."

"You really think he will?" she asked, her blue eyes interested.

I shrugged. "Doubt it. Too mean." I closed my eyes, reliving the moment. "I wish I hadn't promised," I said. "It would be so cool to take on every school bully and creep. Every weak or unpopular kid would have a protector—me."

"Wouldn't that make you a bully?" she asked.

"Not if I'm defending other people," I protested. "Anyway, at lunch meet me at the libe, okay? Before we test the suit I want to look at this week's holo display. Isn't it supposed to be a scene from a science-fiction book instead of one of those planetary landscapes like usual?"

"Someone told me it's from *Dune* and it's really cool," she said.

"Great," I said, rubbing my hands.

At lunch I met Natalie at the library. The holographic display case had a small crowd before it, but we soon got our turn to look. It was indeed a scene from *Dune*. "Wow," I said, staring.

The holograph really was spectacular—the sands seemed to stretch for miles, the sky was a fierce, scoured blue, and the huge sandworm ridden by some tiny Fremen figures looked real enough to give me a shiver.

"So how did the tests go in the park yesterday?" Nat asked. She made a face. "I'm really sorry I couldn't be there." And she sounded like it. In fact she sounded so sorry I couldn't make myself ask why she hadn't come.

I filled her in on the details. At the end she sighed

and said, "What happens when you get done with your experiments?"

"I dunno. My aunt said something about the government. I suppose they'll go nutso over this thing."

"If they're ready," she said.

"Ready?" I squawked as the bell rang. "What's not to be ready for?"

Nat gave me a lopsided smile. "Are most people ready for real changes? Not just a supersuit, but the changes that might come after?"

"Sure," I said.

"For TV phones and hovercars, maybe," Natalie said. "But how about real change—like meeting life from other planets?" She nodded at the holograph display.

"Depends on the aliens, though," I added, hoping to make her laugh. "Not if they look like snot amoebas or cockroaches. Horror city!"

"You think cockroaches are ugly?" Nat asked, her blue eyes round. "I think they're kind of neat—so beautifully designed, and the exoskeleton such a nifty natural protection. It's a great design for an alien."

Had Natalie been so poor she had to make pets of cockroaches when she was little? I winced, looking back at the display—then got my Big Idea.

"Our next test is the lenses," I whispered, making sure no one was listening. "I think I'll do some on the display, right now. No one here will look twice at the helmet—they'll all think it's some lab experiment."

Nat hesitated, then said, "Let me just find out which book they're doing next." She pointed at the display. "Maybe they'll take suggestions."

As she walked away I unzipped my backpack and slid out the helmet. By then everyone was gone from the corridor, so I clicked on the radio.

"Marcos? You there?"

His voice came through clearly. "Aren't you at school?"

"Yup. School library. Chill out—the suit is under my clothes. I thought I'd run the lenses test on the new holograph, but I might have to click off fast if someone comes." I looked around impatiently for Nat, hoping she could at least guard me from possible nosers.

Marcos said, "Hang on a sec—gotta sign off."

"Sign off what?"

"BBS. This laptop has a modem—I was doing a real-time conference with a couple kids on the East Coast."

"Sounds fun," I said, feeling envy. "Don't you ever have to study?"

"Two hours of trig this morning," he said. "And an hour of chem—until it was time for the RTC. Econ and lit I'll do tonight. Why?"

"Because I'm jealous," I said. "All that freedom! Do you miss school?"

"Nah. Yeah. Sometimes," he said. "Ready here."

"Here goes . . . Well, this is a drag," I said a moment later. "The zoom just washes everything out . . . The infrared is kind of neat. It shows where all the heat is—the hidden mechanical stuff, I guess."

"How about the neural-enhancer lens?"

I clicked it on and then blinked at the display. "Whoa—did the power go out? The display has disappeared!" I pulled the lenses up and stared in surprise at the case, which now showed the *Dune* scene intact. "Hey! The neural-clump lens sees right through the holograph," I said, then looked around again for Nat. "I wonder what happened to her?" I muttered.

"Natalie?"

"Yeah. She was right here—then she went inside to ask something, and hasn't come out. Weird."

"Yeah, weird," he said. "Try the neural-clump enhancer on normal stuff."

"Okay. More cat lens, coming up." I looked around the corridor and at the little garden patch in front of the door. "I hate this thing," I said.

"Tell me what you see and feel, so I can write it all down."

"Well, my head feels like it's turned into a balloon, and colors look too bright, and perspective is kind of flat but distant. But the worst of it is the crazy stuff."

"Like?"

I stared straight ahead. "Like knots in the air, almost, and rippling walls; only, it lasts just a second, like I blinked, but I haven't. And when I do blink . . ." I stared at a shrub, which flickered like it had some kind of ghost or spirit hiding in it. Finally I realized the lens was giving me a weird ache behind my eyes, so I clicked it off and sighed with relief.

"We'll have to try it again," he said. "We're getting paid for this."

"Right," I said dismally.

He laughed. "Take a break. Bell should ring soon anyway." And the radio went dead.

With a sense of relief I zipped the helmet into my

pack and went inside the library. I found Nat talking to one of the math teachers. Had Mr. Lopez kept her yakking all that time?

The bell rang before I could ask, but I told Nat before we separated that I'd let her know when the next experiment would be. This time I'd show her the lenses.

"Can hardly wait," she said, grinning.

After school I headed as usual for the bus, but when I saw Knucklebutt and Nerd standing around in front of the bus door glowering at passing students, my feet slowed. I remembered that business about the backpack on the morning ride. Could they be looking for me?

"I dunno," I muttered, "but maybe it's time for another running test."

So I ran. It was great—the suit kept me light and cool. I slowed down only when I realized I was near Marcos's street, and I remembered that I was supposed to go there anyway.

Still, I felt funny as I knocked on his door. A moment later Marcos himself appeared. "Come in," he said, and hit at a control with a flat hand, abruptly turning his chair.

In silence I followed him until we reached a bedroom fitted out with a nifty desk at one end, a bed at the other, and all the wall space between given over to waist-high bookcases. I saw a lot of familiar science-fiction titles there and realized this could be Noah's room, or Jessica's—or mine. Marcos wheeled to the corner by the desk and just looked at me, so I yanked off the helmet and started babbling.

"I, um, thought it might be time for another test, so

I ran. I was a little faster than normal—well, a lot, but not like Superman—but it was hard to keep my balance. Kind of like running downhill."

He nodded, silently pulling his laptop onto a board across the wheelchair arms. Then he started typing.

"I did the lenses on the last block. That cat lens really distorts things. Oh! Want to know something about the infrared?"

He looked up.

I sighed. "This is a groaner, Marcos," I said, feeling my face go hot all over again. "You talk to me great on the radio, but you don't in person. Want me to go outside and use the helmet to report?"

To my surprise, dull red patches appeared in his thin cheeks. "No. It's okay," he said. "What did you see?"

"Well, infrared makes everyone look like a demented modern-art painting—except for Siamese cats. I saw two on your block, and they look just like themselves."

"That's because the dark hair corresponds directly with lower body temp. Cool at head and tail, the rest light—and warm." Then he looked up at me, his dark eyes sober. "I'm not used to you talking to me instead of to the ground, or the sky, or a wall."

It was my turn to get a red face. "I'm sorry," I said. "I just don't want to be, like, *staring*."

He turned away. "That's what most people say. So they listen to my voice and pretend that the rest of me doesn't exist."

I winced. "Most people?"

He shrugged. "Except for the relatives that make sad faces and pat my head and say how they'll always think of me how I was before—the great soccer star. Like this is supposed to make me feel better." Once again he gave me that twisted smile, then he shrugged. "And your friend Natalie. Speaking of Natalie—did she ever come back?"

"Got sidetracked by a math teacher."

He drummed his fingers on his chair arm, then shrugged again. "Let's get busy," he said.

So it looked like everything would be okay. But after a few days passed, life was definitely not okay.

One, Natalie avoided me. I mean, she talked to me at school—wanted to hear everything about the suit—but she still was not able to make any of the experiment times. Marcos started looking squinty-eyed about this. But he wouldn't say why, and I didn't press—I had my own problem, which was also suit related.

My ride on the bus every day was a nightmare. Things stung me in the back of my neck, I was tripped when I got on or off the bus, and of course there were the loud comments and nasty laughter. Worst of all, Knucklebutt and his snickery pal Nerd managed to get some other creeps to join in. I tried ignoring them, but it only seemed to make them worse.

Several times I almost yanked on the gloves so I could *really* test out the suit's powers by stomping those twits, but I didn't. I kept remembering what Tia Nita had said—and besides, I knew that one day (maybe soon) I wouldn't have the suit anymore. I had to solve that mess on my own—or if I couldn't solve it, ride it out.

Well, after a few days of this, Marcos said we'd logged enough time to report to my aunt. I went over to her house from school the next day and found them both there.

From the looks of them, they'd been talking for a while. My aunt asked me a few questions about the suit, then she said, "Has Natalie given you a reason for not being able to help with the experiments?"

"No," I said. "But she is really interested—always wants to hear about it."

They looked at each other.

"What?" I demanded. "What is it?" And a horrible thought occurred: "You don't think she's an industrial spy or something, do you?" I had to laugh at the idea. "*Can* kids gets jobs as spies? Or . . . do you think it's her parents?"

"Maybe it's time for all of us to talk to her," Tia Nita said calmly. "I'll explain everything myself. Invite her over, okay?"

I agreed.

Next morning, Knucklebutt and Nerd were meaner than ever—and not just to me. By the time I got off that bus, I felt like a thunderstorm was about to break, right on my head.

Natalie was in the usual place, watching the kids get off the bus. When I got near her, for once she didn't seem to notice me. I turned to see what she was staring at—and saw those two senior creeps slouching away toward the classrooms.

"Tia Nita wants you to come over," I said, figuring the suit was more important than watching Knucklebutt and his idiot friend.

Natalie turned to me. "To do what?"

"To talk about the suit," I said. And as she stared at me in silence, I added, "And I guess to ask you some questions."

Natalie tipped her head back as though listening, then looked at me. "If you're really serious about this, then meet me at the dump at five."

"That's it?" I squawked, just as the bell rang. "The *dump?* What's going *on?* And why does everyone know but me?"

She waved and disappeared in the rush of students.

Ten to five found me on my bike and moving fast.

There's not much to say about a dump, except that it's dirty and dangerous. Ours is near a freeway interchange, where everyone throws their old fridges and old cars and the like. No one but rats and gangs hangs out there—and if you ask me, the rats are less of a problem.

"I still think we ought to have told your aunt about this," Marcos said over the radio as I glanced back at the skyline. The sunset looked red and mean.

"I have to know what's going on first," I muttered, eyeing the rundown buildings looming ahead. "Nat's my friend. And if this is what it takes—"

Marcos sighed. "I think there's more going on here than we can handle."

"Like what?" I demanded. "You keep saying you're suspicious but you won't tell me why. And if you think she's a spy, I'll tell you right now that I've spent hours and hours talking with her about everything from Roman history to rock music, and I think if she was secretly working for some sinister idea-stealing gangster I'd have gotten a *little* hint of it."

Marcos sighed. "It's not what she says, or does, it's what she doesn't do. She's—different. I've learned to observe. Can't do much else." He ended on a wry note that didn't fool me anymore.

"Look," I said, "if it turns out you're right and I'm wrong, I'll listen from now on. But right now, let me do this my way, okay?" As I finished, I realized I was hinting that we'd still be talking after the experiment—that we'd be friends. My face burned, and I waited for his *no way*—which didn't come. So I said, "Stop blabbing! If someone is going to bop me one I'd rather hear it first."

I kept riding along, scanning both sides, until I spotted Natalie's silhouette perched near the top of a big wall of smashed cars. She was completely alone. I stopped, used my zoom to make certain it really was her, then parked my bike—hoping it would be there when I got back.

The suit made it slightly easier to climb up those cars, though if I bounded too high I lost my balance. "Natalie?" I called. "Nat?"

To my surprise, she put her finger to her lips.

" 'Be quiet'?" I whispered, clambering up near her. "In the dump? Like we might disturb someone studying?" But she didn't laugh. "Why're we here?"

"Because you don't see, or when you do, you don't understand what it is you're seeing . . ." She sighed.

"Are you talking about the suit?"

"Come on." She climbed up the car stack again, all the way to the top. When she got there, she lay flat and peered down at the other side.

Not knowing what to think anymore, I just followed along. Then when I got a look at what was going on in the valley of car wrecks beyond us, once again I got whacked with a total shock.

I mean, in a way it was what I expected to find in the dump—a bunch of mean-looking guys taking turns beating up three other guys. They even had their own flashlights, so they could see where they were punching. But two of the three guys they were trashing were instantly familiar: my old pals Knucklebutt and Nerd.

"Practical jokers," she whispered, pointing down at Knucklebutt. "Most of their victims don't fight back. These others do—but only when they'll win." She turned to me. "So? What do we do?"

I shook my head. "Wow. Alice in Wonderland had it easy. Did you think I'd run away? Or laugh? And why should it matter?"

"Everyone matters," she said. And before I could open my mouth she reached down to a big stack of pancaked hubcaps, picked up two, and with two flicks of her wrist she sent them sailing down just like Frisbees.

Poink! Clank! They smacked right into the chests of the two guys just stepping up to take a swing at Knucklebutt's sagging body.

"How did she know?" I muttered.

Marcos said in my ear, "No idea. But one thing's for sure, she's even a better observer than I am."

Well, by now I felt I'd dropped into some kind of crazy movie. Remembering the power of the suit, I reached down, carefully picked up a stack of hubcaps, hoping ragged edges wouldn't cut my gloves, and then I whizzed a rain of steel pizzas on the gang below. Curses and yells echoed up, and two of the guys started climbing toward us.

I realized who had the protective suit and who had just bare flesh, so I said to Nat, "Hide! I'll draw them off." Then I stood up and waggled my fingers by my ears. "Hi, bozos!" I screeched. "You must be real tough if it takes eleven to jump three!"

"Hey! You little—" The closest guy was drowned out almost immediately by insults from the rest.

I jumped down toward them, turning a flip in the air before I landed—right between the creeps holding up Knucklebutt & Friends. A shove here, a kick there, and the three were standing alone, staring at me.

"Run," I yelled in their faces. "Now!"

Meanwhile the rest of the gang decided to stop shouting and start charging. I jumped right over the heads of the first three and landed in the midst of the others. I was no longer afraid—the suit protected me, and I felt great. "I'm your worst nightmare!" I howled.

Four or five of them socked me—at least I felt the suit flash warmth—so I spun around with my fists out, connecting with chins and arms and stomachs, and heard satisfying "Ow!"s and "Oof!"s.

I also heard the snick of a switchblade.

"Lights," Natalie said—she was right behind me.

"Run, Nat," I yelled, kicking a flashlight out of a guy's hand. The beam arced weirdly around and around, a kaleidoscope of blue light, then smashed against the ground. A second or so later, I smashed the other one as well. It was now totally dark. "Lights gone!"

"You're crazy," Marcos said in my ear. Then, "Remember your infrared."

I clicked it on, saw red body shapes converging. I shoved a few away—then stumbled over a fender. Cold metal junk didn't show up in that lens, so I went back to the clear one. By now my eyes had adjusted. So had theirs, of course—but I was a lot faster as I leapt back up the junker-car wall, then down the other side. A quick switch to the infrared showed the guys rapidly coming after me. A cold, brief glint from the lights on the freeway shone on knives.

"Uh-oh," I muttered, and started running toward the freeway overpass.

The creepazoids fanned out, trying to encircle me, but I was too fast. Babbling a constant report to Marcos, I ran under the freeway—and almost dead-ended at a sheer cement wall. Veering sharply in the darkness, I ran for the on-ramp.

"Infrared!" Marcos yelled.

I obeyed, saw the waiting figure just in time. Heavy hands grabbed at my arms. I snapped free, using my momentum to bound right up onto the overpass. "Okay, I think I've shaken 'em. I just hope Nat got away safe— Uh-oh. Incoming."

Four or five of the creeps had raced up the on-ramp and were coming at me. I gulped, turned, and ran straight into the oncoming traffic. "Here goes nothing," I quavered, and jumped high as the first car zoomed under my feet. Another raced by and I dodged it, stumbling back—straight into the path of a big, roaring—

"Truck," I croaked.

"FLAT!" Marcos yelled, and I flung myself down on the cement moments before four big sets of tires thudded over me.

The suit flashed hot four times, toasting my back,

and went as stiff as a diving suit. Then I jumped up and nearly flew into the air.

"Are they gone?" Marcos asked.

"They're gone," a familiar voice said behind me: Natalie!

"Come on," she said.

We ran down an off-ramp and up a quiet street. And though the suit was brimming with energy, which made me sprint at Olympic speed, she kept up without even looking sweaty.

We stopped at a little park, and I faced Natalie, my hands on my hips. Though my radio was still on, Marcos was silent. "Okay, first thing," I said. "How did you know those other creeps were planning to jump them? How did you know those were the guys I told you about? And why save them?"

"I watch and I listen to everything," Nat said, then rubbed her eyes. "But it's not enough to enable me to understand it." She dropped her hands. "I had to know what you'd do with all that power when it was not you being attacked."

Marcos whistled.

"Stop that," I muttered, then to Nat I said hastily, "Uh, not you. Natalie, I don't get it. Were you, like, testing me?"

And to my astonishment, she nodded. "Yes—as I was being tested. Not by you." She smiled. "There are many of us, all learning, talking, watching, trying to understand . . ."

"This makes no sense," I wailed. "You're one of the most understanding kids I know. You're so nice to everybody—and they like you back!"

She reached out, touched my helmet. "Marisa, I'd like to come back, but I know I won't be welcome until you can live with each other."

"Me? And those two fathead seniors?"

"You and the rest of your people."

I opened my mouth, about to remind her of all the different kinds of people in our club. Chinese, African-American, Hispanic, Russian Jew—none of it really mattered to us. Except—

"People," I repeated slowly. "You don't mean just the club."

"I think it's bigger than that," Marcos said in my ear.

And, as if she'd heard him, Nat murmured, "Bigger."

"The school?"

"Bigger. Much bigger." She threw her arms wide.

"Like—the world?" I laughed.

And so did she. On the radio, I could hear Marcos breathing.

"*Your* world," she said. "Look at me, Marisa, the real me, and tell me if I'm still your friend. No—use your cat lens, the one that sees through holomasks."

Slowly I switched lenses, and then stared.

"I knew it," Marcos muttered. "Marisa—tell me what you see!"

But I couldn't. My voice had gone dry.

Gone was the girl with the round blue eyes, and in her place was a gleaming carapace, antennae, chelae—a big blue ant. And from the ant came Natalie's voice.

"Okay, superhero." She laughed. "Now what?"

NANCY SPRINGER

WE DON'T KNOW WHY

So me'n Kris were basically out atmosphere cruising in our solar wings, flying fast and low to the planet surface, kinda looking for trouble to get into because there was really nothing to do. It was a stupid planet, boringly Earth-like—just a little more gravity, squatty trees, lumpy stumpy animals that made us laugh, the way they scuttled away from us. The wings didn't flap or fold or or anything, they were just your standard helio-energized antigravity foils, but anything was better than staying on board and listening to my father lecture me about how I was lucky to be young and alive and I ought to shape up.

"Stop it, Mishell!" Kris yelled at me.

I stalled a little because he had startled me. "Stop what?"

"Thinking!" He swooped so low his chrome boots rattled a treetop. "So your brother's dead, so what," he complained. "Everybody dies sometime." Kris was totally heartless and rude, which was why I had started going out with him. His coolness was a lot easier to take than sympathy, and Kris was totally cool. He never wore a helmet in atmosphere. Said he liked the feel of all those little air molecules in his mane of platinum hair. He had more hair than I did, and I was the captain's daughter, but that was part of how Kris was cool. Nobody could tell him how to act or what to do. I didn't wear my helmet anymore either, unless I needed it for oxygen.

"Bet you can't goose a goose," Kris said as a riverside meadow full of some kind of waterfowl came into view. All facing away from us and making simpleminded noises through their bills, they had their heads down—they seemed to be eating the new spring grass. Maybe they really were geese, though on this planet they looked as short necked as ducks, with wings that were oversized, big, and clumsy compared to the rest of them—like mine.

"Go ahead," Kris challenged. "Try it."

Sneak up behind one of those downy waddling bird butts, he meant, and startle it silly. Scare them all silly.

The solar wings were featherweight and shining and dead silent, like riding on light. If Kris would stop flapping his big mouth, it actually might be possible for me to glide down and goose a goose.

Unless I caught a wingtip on the ground, in which case I would probably be killed. But I didn't care. Since Mykel had died I really didn't care about anything.

"Shut up," I whispered at Kris as I kicked my booted feet up to slant my body downward.

He didn't shut up. "Uh-oh," I heard him say in bored tones as one of my six-meter wings scraped against some tree fingers and threw me out of control.

I nosedived into geese flying up with a frightened clamor like they were a chorus for my panic. "Help me!" I cried to Kris.

"No way," I heard him say, distantly—he had turned his back on me, was flying away. "Are you crazy?"

I managed to throw myself sideways, turning my dive into a spin, a spiral that lessened the impact somewhat. Still, I don't remember much. Just a major quaking resonance through my whole body. Then blackness.

My head hurt like a drum somebody was beating on when I woke up in a shadowy place full of soft lights. I blinked. Very different than the quick, hard lights on board. These lights seemed to breathe, like live things, yet they were so timid and dim that I could scarcely see the—people?

Behind each light, a sun-darkened face, a stumpy body. I had not known there were people on this planet. Neither had anyone on board, I guess. That was what we were here for, orbiting out of sight behind the clouds, to find out. The scanners had just been setting up to look and listen before Kris and I sneaked out.

These short sun-browned people were not much like me. Generations in artificial gee and artificial light had made spacefarers like me willowy and pale. But the bilateral symmetry was unmistakable, the two-eyed faces, the two hands holding the—candles? Yeah, candles. I recognized the lights now from the Earthtime narratives. And I recognized that these were primitive humans.

That didn't mean I wasn't afraid of them. The more primitive humans were, the less broadly they defined *human*. These people might not recognize me as one of them at all. My heart started to pound, and I sat up.

There was a gasp, then a hush as if no one was breathing. Nobody moved, including me.

But then one candle moved. It separated itself from the ranks and wavered toward me. Above and behind it I could make out the hairless face of a strong old man, a grandfather, a patriarch, a—chief? Lord? Secretary of the interior? The glinting, elaborate apparel on his head might have been a warrior's bonnet or a crown. I should have worn my helmet after all. Aside from saving my stupid, aching head, its mass and orichalc gleam would have impressed this dignitary. Yet he did not approach me with any of the condescension I had come to expect from men in large hats. He came forward slowly, with a measured, formal tread, and in the stillness of his face I saw—fear?

He bowed his head. Knelt before me.

Only then did I realize that I had been lying on a

raised—something. Dais? The candles all flickered as everyone knelt.

The headdressed man said something, but I could not understand, not having a languagetran with me. Eye contact, gestures might have helped some, but he spoke with his head tilted down, his eyes staring at the floor or maybe even closed—I could not tell. Was he speaking to me? It didn't feel like he was talking to me at all, but nobody else was there. And then he shifted his candle to one hand and picked up something from the floor with the other. Blindly he stretched his arm toward me, offering—

Bread?

Brown loaves, dark and crusty as if they had been baked in ashes or something, definitely not a product of the electric simulator ovens on board. Even if I had been hungry, normally I wouldn't have eaten such unsanitary-looking bread. But if I wanted to keep these humans happy, I knew, it would be a good idea to take one. I reached. There was a sigh, a murmur, as people began breathing again. I broke my little brown loaf in half, separated a mouthful with my fingers, and found that my hand was shaking. I ate. It wasn't bad. All the time I was eating the big-hat man stayed where he was, on his knees—reverent, that was the word. Or no, not just reverent. Awed. They all seemed hushed with awe.

Should have made me feel good, right? But it didn't. I didn't want their damn awe. Chewing the tough bread made my head hurt worse than ever—every part of me hurt—and I was still in my boots and titanium torso panels and wings, big clumsy things battered by the crash—I wanted somebody to help me take them off, and after that all I wanted in the world was a hot shower and maybe some soup and a soft place to sleep and somebody, a mother—right, like I had a mother—to tuck me in.

None of it was going to happen. I lay down where I was.

The next thing I knew, it was light. There was warm light pouring into the—shadowy place? Yeah, it was the same place, the same stubby people. The shadows had been night, a primitive night dark as a cave, but now day streamed down, all—colors? Sunlight, through tall glass windows between ribbed stone arches—I had heard about places like this. They had brought me to a sanctuary of their culture, a haven of light where they burned candles by night, and where by day the windows glowed with prismatic colors arranged to form bright pictures.

Pictures of—

Kris?

I sat straight up and stared—that is, I had to close my eyes until my head cleared, and then I gawked. Each window glorified a tall, willowy, pale being with wings that shone like white fire. A mane of sun-colored hair. A blaze of light around the body. Chest plates on some of them, long white robes on others. Some flying, some standing—but details didn't matter. My gaze caught on their grave faces, their wise wild eyes, their aureoles, their wings.

No. Not Kris. Kris had never had such eyes. These were pictures of—what was the word?

Someone was crying. I looked, and there was a

woman kneeling before me with a dying child in her arms.

My heart turned over. The child, a tiny girl presented to me in a dress fit for a bride—there were big insects of some kind crawling on her frail face, and she was so weak she didn't move to brush them off. She seemed barely conscious. Some sort of wasting illness—her tawny skin was stretched dry and hot over her bones. The mother crouched there weeping, a short sturdy woman with her smooth dark hair parted in the middle. That was all I could see, the very straight part in her hair, she bowed her head so low. What did she want of me? What did she think I was, a doctor?

A—what was the word—an angel?

I had to get out of there. I swung my feet down and stood up. Wobbled a little, but I made it. Braced myself against the—altar? Grabbed some more bread and some of the fruit piled there. My head didn't feel too awful now, after more sleep, though my body felt highly unreliable. I tottered down the steps of my platform, then hung on to the benches—there were rows of benches with backs—and walked out. The place was full of people who parted widely to let me through but then followed me at a distance. I could feel them gazing at me, at my pale hair haloed in the light of the aspiring windows, at my shining torso panels, at my shining flight foils that looked like wings.

They had brought me here—to this cathedral of angels—because they thought that was what I was.

And then they had brought me a child to heal.

What should I do? I would have saved the child if I could, but I didn't know how. Should I try anyway?

Lay on hands? No, that was stupid, I would be totally faking it.

I *was* totally faking it. Should I take off my equipment? But if they knew the truth, they might kill me.

I did nothing. I did not even walk away for long. Outside there was nothing to hold on to, and I couldn't get far before my knees started to give way. I sat down on the grass.

This was a hilltop sanctuary. Down below were a village, a river in spring flood, people netting fish from the shore and pulling dead leaves out of gardens and going about their business. I guess they had to do that, even though there was an angel watching. Somebody had to fix supper. Life had to go on.

The river leapt and rippled like a lizard. Geese flew over in a V, crying to the sky. The crying woman with the dying child sat down some distance from me. Other people sat down with her, very quietly, making a large circle, a halo of people, around me.

"I wish I could talk with you," I said.

They gazed back at me with fear and probably some resentment, probably wondering; Why hadn't I saved the little girl? Nobody smiled. Even the babies were silent. I looked mostly at the babies and the children as I ate my bread and my fruit, and the little ones were not afraid to look back at me, their dark eyes wide and sober in their small faces.

"Don't ever die," I said to them.

I remembered Mykel, though his eyes had been not wide and dark, but gray and sharp like mine. My father and I would never know exactly what had happened, just that something had ruptured. There was no hope of finding a body; there would be no ashes to scatter in space. I hated the universe for Mykel's sake. I hated everything.

Except these people and their dark-eyed babies. I guess I didn't hate them.

I heard cries, and I thought for an instant that it was the yelping geese. But then the cries rose to screams, and I saw down below—two boys in a frail splinter of a boat, midriver. Stupid, stupid—what were they doing on that killer water? Paddling hard, they were fighting their way toward shore, but the river was turning them broadside to the current. And the river was far stronger than they would ever be. They could not fight it, they would be swept away—like Mykel had been swept away from me—

I was on my feet, screaming, the way the villagers down below were screaming. Without thinking, not even knowing whether my wings were still functioning, I thumbed the power recess on my chest panel. I shot into the air. An instant later I lashed my body around so that I dove toward the river.

It was crazy. Insane. I had no idea when my wings might fail. Still, I reached the frail boat, where two terrified faces looked up at me. I don't know whether the boys were more frightened of the river or of me. I grabbed the one nearest to me under his armpits just as the boat rolled sideways and filled with water. It was all I could do to lift him—he was a lot shorter than I am, but a lot denser, and the gravity was fierce on this planet. Somehow I found strength. Maybe their food had given me strength. His feet almost dragged in the water as I lugged him toward shore. "Help, get the other one!" I shouted as if someone could be there, Kris maybe, someone who had wings and could pluck fool boys from water. But there was no one to help but me.

I dumped the boy in the mud at the shoreline, where half a dozen villagers reached out for him, and I wheeled and darted after the other one. Babble of voices behind me was lost in the clamor of the river. I saw the belly of the boat as it floated downriver like a dead fish, and near it I saw a head shining like a small dark sun. I thumbed for more power, flew faster, nearly out of control, but before I could reach the boy he disappeared in roiling water as the river narrowed to a deep, gushing ravine. If my wings caught in the trees to either side of that strait, I would crash, that would be it for me.

I had thought I didn't care about anything, but I did. I wanted to live.

Yet I flew in there anyway, because even more than life I wanted— Somehow this boy was Mykel . . . Just as I knew I would have to give him up I spotted him again. His arm lifted toward me. I swooped and grabbed. The water dragged at us as I thumbed for even more power—but there was no more power. I needed more strength—I didn't have it. I knew I was not going to be able to save us both.

I hung on anyway. Struggled upward and got him mostly out of the water. Flew wildly, veering downriver with the rushing water pushing his legs along until an elbow of rock jutted from the shore. I aimed him there. Dropped him safely out of the water, but I could not tell whether he was alive. Felt a wing crumple into the steep bank, and knew I was going to die—

But at that moment I felt the Columbuscraft transport beam latch onto me. The last thing I saw on that planet was people running toward me along the top of the ravine. "Good-bye," I called to them as I vanished.

The next moment I stood in the entry portal of the ship, where the captain, my father, was waiting to debrief me. And, probably, to throw a hissy fit.

Usually when I had to face my father I put on a protective armor of attitude: straight spine, hard face, silence. But there was no time for any of that. Or maybe I forgot.

"He's dead," I said.

"Are you all right?" my father said at the same time, which was not like him. "Get those things off her," he said to the techs who were already working as fast as they could to remove my gear.

"I couldn't save him," I said.

"There's a big bruise and a clot of dried blood on your head," my father said. "Why weren't you wearing your helmet? Why were you out there at all? With Kris, of all people. He's no damn good, Mishell."

"I couldn't save him," I said.

But he was adjusting one earpiece of his ever-present headset, with his listening look on his face. "The boy in the water? You did save him," he said. He knew all about it. Probably had been watching me the whole time. "The languagetrans are picking up clear signals on the scanners. He's alive."

I shook my head. "Mykel," I said.

He stiffened, looking back at me.

"Why?" I asked. "Why couldn't there have been somebody to save him? Or something?"

Then I stood staring at him, I was so startled to see

tears in his eyes. We hadn't talked about Mykel before. I hadn't wanted to.

He stretched his hand toward me. He said, very low, "We don't know why things happen, Mishell. We just don't know."

I had to close my eyes. Didn't see him step toward me, but I did feel him hug me. My arms lifted and I hung on to him, I laid my head against the rock of his shoulder as he hugged me hard. It was maybe a whole minute before he turned into his cranky self again and started hustling me toward sick bay.

A while later, tucked in by a nurse with a firm hand, I should have been sleeping, but I was lying there in the dim blue light listening to the laserharp music, awake but having dreams like visions—maybe from the drugs. Maybe not. I dreamed of the people on the planet far below. *Angel,* they were saying. *The angel sat with us and ate our bread.* In a couple of generations, an old man would tell his grandchildren how in his youth he had been rescued by an angel. *The angel rescued me,* he would say, *but not my sister. My sister died. The angel would not save her. When I was a boy, the angel rescued me from drowning,* he would say. *And she rescued my friend. We knew we were special ones, blessed ones, with angels to protect us. We grew tall. But one day when he was still a young man my friend went out hunting deer and was captured by the barbarians who live beyond the mountains. And he did not try to escape, but waited in utmost faith for his angel to come and save him and punish the barbarians. His captors tortured him with fire, and no angel came. They tortured him until he died in agony. I know, because I saw. No angel saved him. And I could not save him either.*

We do not know why angels come sometimes and sometimes turn their backs and fly away, the old man would say. *We just don't know. Things happen, and we don't know why.*

ABOUT THE AUTHORS

DAN BENNETT works as a writer and editor for a national computer magazine based in Burlingame, California. His stories have appeared in *The Twilight Zone Magazine* and *A Wizard's Dozen*. He shares a one-bedroom apartment with a formidable computer and an even more formidable black cat.

DEBORAH COATES was raised on a New York dairy farm, attended Cornell University, and went on to graduate school in New Hampshire, before eventually moving to where she now lives with a very large dog named Riley. "Flyboy," her first published science fiction story, is one of a series of tales she's written about Flyboy and Cisco.

DEBRA DOYLE and JAMES D. MACDONALD, an Ivy League Ph.D. and an ex-naval officer respectively, have been married since 1978 and writing together since 1986. Since then they have published many books, including the fantasy novel *Knight's Wyrd,* a series of middle-grade novels known collectively as *Circle of Magic,* and the Mageworlds space opera series: *The Price of the Stars, Starpilot's Grave, By Honor Betray'd,* and *The Gathering Flame.*

GREGORY FEELEY has published science fiction and fantasy stories in a number of magazines and anthologies, including *Weird Tales from Shakespeare, Dinosaur Fantastic,* and *Alternate Outlaws*. He is the author of one science fiction novel, *The Oxygen Barons,* and will soon publish another. "Ursa Minor" is his first story for younger readers.

JOY OESTREICHER has at one time or another worked as a secretary, tariff clerk, administrator, research assistant, dress designer, tailor, shipping clerk, photographer's aide, astrologer, model, and Girl Scout leader. In her spare moments, she has managed to edit *Air Fish,* an anthology, and the poetry magazine *Xenophilia* and to raise her 2.5 children and 2 cats.

JANNI LEE SIMNER was born on Long Island, escaped to St. Louis, and finally ended up in Tucson, Arizona, where she works for the University of Arizona and spends too much of her spare time hiking. She has published more than a dozen stories in many magazines and anthologies, including *Bruce Coville's Book of Nightmares*.

WILL SHETTERLY has written six fantasy novels, including *Elsewhere* and *Nevernever,* and the forthcoming *Dogland*. He and his wife, the novelist Emma Bull, have edited a series of short-story anthologies set in the magical world of Liavek. He is also the publisher of Steel Dragon Inc., which issues limited-edition books, comic books, and recordings of the rock band Cats Laughing and the Flash Girls. He lives in Minneapolis.

SHERWOOD SMITH began making books when she was only five years old, taping paper towels together and illustrating the stories with crayons. She has gone on to write and publish many popular books, including the young adult trilogy *Wren to the Rescue, Wren's Quest,* and *Wren's War,* and, with Dave Trowbridge, the science-fiction adventure series *Exordium* (see below).

MARTHA SOUKUP once portrayed a giant squirrel in a play but thinks of herself primarily as a writer. Her work debuted in *Universe 16,* and she has since published stories in *Asimov's Science Fiction Magazine, Science Fiction Age,* and many anthologies, including *Full Spectrum 4* and *Xanadu 2.* A literally small collection of three of her stories, *Rosemary's Brain,* was published in 1992, and in 1994 one of her stories was made into a short film for Showtime. She has won the Nebula Award and has been a finalist for the Hugo and World Fantasy awards. She lives in San Francisco.

NANCY SPRINGER is the author of sixteen novels, ten children's books, a collection of stories, two poetry collections, and numerous short works. She is the author of the bestselling *The White Hart* and the award-winning children's book *Colt,* as well as the more recent young adult novels *Toughing It*, winner of the Edgar Award, and *Looking for Jamie Bridger.* She lives with her family in Dallastown, Pennsylvania, and spends her spare time teaching, horseback riding, playing violin, and working as a volunteer for an organization for the disabled.

DAVE TROWBRIDGE is the co-author, with Sherwood Smith, of the five novels that make up the science-fiction series *Exordium: The Phoenix in Flight, Ruler of Naught, A Prison Unsought, The Rifter's Covenant,* and *The Thrones of Kronos.* He also works as a writer and editor at a computer trade magazine, and lives in Tujunga, California, near the Angeles National Forest, with three dogs who enjoy hiking and four cats who do not. "Suraki," which is set in the universe of the *Exordium* novels, is his first short story.

LAWRENCE WATT-EVANS grew up in Massachusetts, where at the age of eight he began writing science fiction. Since then he has written many popular novels, including the six novels of the Ethshar fantasy series beginning with *The Misenchanted Sword.* His most recent work is the Three Worlds trilogy: *Out of this World, In the Empire of Shadow,* and *The Reign of the Brown Magician.* He, his wife, his two children, a parakeet, a cat, and about three thousand vintage comic books all share a house in Maryland, in the Washington, D.C., area.

JANE YOLEN is the award-winning author of more than one hundred and fifty books, including *The Wild Hunt, Here There Be Dragons,* and *Here There Be Unicorns.* She has received the World Fantasy Award and the Mythopoeic Society Aslan Award, as well as several of the highest awards in children's literature, including the Regina Medal and the Kerlan Award. She and her husband divide their time between homes in Massachusetts and St. Andrews, Scotland.